T0259944

Learn Ionic 2

Develop Multi-platform Mobile Apps

Joyce Justin
Joseph Jude

Apress®

Learn Ionic 2: Develop Multi-platform Mobile Apps

Joyce Justin
Bangalore, Karnataka, India

Joseph Jude
Panchkula, Haryana, India

ISBN-13 (pbk): 978-1-4842-2616-2
https://doi.org/10.1007/978-1-4842-2617-9

ISBN-13 (electronic): 978-1-4842-2617-9

Library of Congress Control Number: 2017938595

Managing Director: Welmoed Spahr
Lead Editor: Celestin Suresh John
Technical Reviewer: Jayakarthik Jayabalan
Editorial Board: Steve Anglin, Pramila Balan, Laura Berendson, Aaron Black, Louise Corrigan, Jonathan Gennick, Robert Hutchinson, Celestin Suresh John, Nikhil Karkal, James Markham, Susan McDermott, Matthew Moodie, Natalie Pao, Gwenan Spearing
Coordinating Editor: Prachi Mehta
Development Editor: James Markham
Copy Editor: Lori Jacobs
Compositor: SPi Global
Indexer: SPi Global
Artist: SPi Global

Distributed to the book trade worldwide by Springer Science+Business Media New York, 233 Spring Street, 6th Floor, New York, NY 10013. Phone 1-800-SPRINGER, fax (201) 348-4505, e-mail orders-ny@springer-sbm.com, or visit www.springeronline.com. Apress Media, LLC is a California LLC and the sole member (owner) is Springer Science + Business Media Finance Inc (SSBM Finance Inc). SSBM Finance Inc is a **Delaware** corporation.

For information on translations, please e-mail rights@apress.com, or visit www.apress.com.

Apress and friends of ED books may be purchased in bulk for academic, corporate, or promotional use. eBook versions and licenses are also available for most titles. For more information, reference our Special Bulk Sales–eBook Licensing web page at www.apress.com/bulk-sales.

Any source code or other supplementary materials referenced by the author in this text are available to readers at www.apress.com. For detailed information about how to locate your book's source code, go to www.apress.com/source-code/. Readers can also access source code at SpringerLink in the Supplementary Material section for each chapter.

Printed on acid-free paper

Contents

About the Authors

Joyce Justin is a technical lead in IBM MobileFirst™ Platform Development; in her current role, she leads the Push Engine development. Prior to this, she was working with customers on various IBM products. She has been a speaker at multiple conferences, has received several IBM technical awards, and has patents to her credit.

Joseph Jude has worked in the IT (information technology) field for more than 20 years. During this time he has played multiple roles as a CTO, architect, and business analyst. Joseph is currently serving as a Chief Technology Officer (CTO) of NetSolutions, a boutique IT services company. Prior to that, he was a consultant to the Ministry of Corporate Affairs, India. During this time he architected an e-governance solution for LLP Act, managed an MCA21 e-governance project, and oversaw integration of MCA21 system with other e-governance systems. He regularly blogs at www.jjude.com.

Acknowledgments

No book is an island. This book is no different. We would like to take a moment to thank those who made this book possible.

Without the visionary folks at Ionic this book would not have been possible. Thank you all.

We want to thank everyone at Apress for bringing this book into the world. We only interacted with Suresh John, Prachi Mehta, and James Markham; but we are sure there were countless others who worked tirelessly without caring if anyone thanked them. Thank you all.

A special thanks to our technical reviewer, Jayakarthik Jayabalan, who managed to review all the chapters on time, despite being stuck in heavy Chennai floods.

Joseph

I want to thank my dad for showing that hard work and discipline pays off in the long term; my mom for loving me like only a mom can love, especially when I struggled to build my life; my sister for being a friend, advisor, and co-author; my wife for being a queen of our home (true to her name) and building it, while I locked myself into a room pretending to write; my kids for refreshing me whenever I felt tired.

I want to thank Sastry Tumuluri, a dear friend and a mentor, for being a driving force behind all my career breaks. I owe him a lot more than just thanks in a book.

One last thank you. Twenty-six years ago, I accepted Jesus as the Lord. Ever since then, He has renewed my mind, guided me in every venture, and been with me and made me lucky. Thank you Lord.

Joyce

As they say, the family is always a great place for learning, I would like to thank my father for teaching me that hard work pays; my mother for being an inspiration and motivation; my brother for being there for me always; my husband for being patient with all my tantrums and being supportive of all the work that I do, including this book; my daughter for making me smile when I need it most.

I want to thank Vinod Kumar KG and Vijaya Bhaskar Siddareddi for being my mentors and guiding me throughout my career.

This acknowledgement would not be complete without thanking my beautiful friends Subhashini Raman and Gayathiri Bheemesh for motivating me to write this book.

A final thank you to God for being the light and showing me the path.

The original version of this book was revised. An erratum to this book can be found at
https://doi.org/10.1007/978-1-4842-2617-9_10

CHAPTER 1

■ ■ ■

Welcome to the World of Ionic

The Ionic team has built a strong ecosystem around its framework. The framework and the ecosystem have reinforced each other to establish a stable hybrid mobile development framework.

Learning Objectives

- Reason for hybrid mobile application development
- Advantages of Ionic over other hybrid mobile application development platforms

Exploding Opportunity

There are 2.5 billion smart phones in the world, and that number is growing at an exponential rate. As a mobile developer, that's the number of devices on which your application can possibly find a place. But, these smart phones are not homogeneous. At the operating system (OS) level, there are only two popular OSs—Android and iOS. However, these devices come in more than ten different screen sizes. Designing and coding user interfaces that work well across so many screen sizes is a huge challenge for mobile application developers.

This challenge must be combined with growing customer expectations. Customers expect applications to work the same across their devices. They also expect regular updates to the application, indicating the commitment of the developers.

Finding developers who know a particular language (e.g., Swift or Java) is easy. But training them to use debug tools and instrumentation tools for each of the mobile platforms is a tough job for any product managerin any enterprise.

Hybrid mobile development platforms provide a welcome relief from the difficulties these challenges present. These platforms come in two kinds. Most of them are built on top of web technologies like HTMLS5, CSS3, and JavaScript. Platforms like Ionic and Appcelerator fall into this category. Then there is Xamarin, which is built on top of .Net technology. All of these tools help the developers to move into mobile application development using their existing knowledge.

Ionic has emerged as a popular multiplatform framework. for many reasons, among them

- **Tools & Services**: Ionic provides a range of tools and services that eases development. There are powerful command-line tools to create the new Ionic application, to generate appropriately sized icons for each platform, to serve the app on a web browser, and so on. Ionic Playground is a tool to learn Ionic without installing anything on your computer. Ionic View is an application through which you can distribute your app to testers and clients for early feedback.

© Josephine Eskaline Joyce Justin and Joesph Xavier Judes 2017
J. Justin and J. Jude, *Learn Ionic 2*, https://doi.org/10.1007/978-1-4842-2617-9_1

- **Documentation**: Ionic has concise but comprehensive documentation on its main site. The documentation details the essentials of the framework—installing, starting, testing, and pushing to the stores. Reading through the documentation will allow you to learn all about Ionic, which is also the first topic of the documentation.

- **Community**: Despite clear documentation, developers, run into irritating bugs from time to time. Members in the online community help us resolve them and move further in our development. Ionic has an active and growing community (105,613 users as we write this). Since, Ionic is based on Angularjs, Angularjs communities support Ionic developers too.

- **Rich marketplace**: Do you want to integrate with Stripe payment gateway, or with Google maps? Or, do you want to style with the latest Google material design? Ionic has you covered with its marketplace, where there are paid as well as free themes, plug-ins, and starter apps.

- **Free and Open Source**: Ionic framework is MIT-licensed open source software. This means you can use Ionic to build and sell personal as well as enterprise applications without paying any fee to anyone.

Ionic's Approach to Building Multiplatform Mobile Apps

Ionic is a HTML5 framework that stands on the shoulders of HTML5, CSS3, Cordova, and Angularjs. Figure 1-1 shows the high-level view of Ionic application architecture.

Figure 1-1. Ionic application architecture

Native software development kits (SDKs) from the respective platforms (iOS and Android) still form the basis of the entire Ionic framework. Cordova, through its plug-ins, exposes device capabilities like accelerometer, camera, and contacts to Ionic. Ionic exposes native-styled mobile controls, like textbox and labels. It also handles any user interface (UI) interactions, like tap and type, with these controls.

Since Ionic is based on web technologies, you develop Ionic apps using HTML5, CSS3, and JavaScript. Ionic uses AngularJs for its core functionality. Developers are not required to use AngularJs to write their apps, but it is recommended. In this book, we will be using AngularJs to build mobile apps.

Summary

The Ionic framework helps us to build multiplatform mobile applications with our existing knowledge of web technologies. We also saw why it is an excellent framework in this category of tools.

In the next chapter, we will build a simple mobile application using the Ionic framework.

CHAPTER 2

Build Your First Ionic App

In this chapter we'll build a simple counter app. The app will have just two buttons: one to increment the counter and another to reset it.

Learning Objectives

- How to install Ionic 2
- Types of templates Ionic provides to quick-start your development
- How to create a new Ionic 2 application using the template
- Folder structure for a typical Ionic 2 project
- How to run the app in a browser

What We Will Build

An app with just two buttons sounds so simple. Let us add a few more details. If you close and reopen the app, the app should reset the counter to 0. If the app is sent to background and brought back to the foreground, the counter should retain the previous value.

Now it looks like a good enough app to start with Ionic 2. Let us dive into building it.

Installing Ionic 2

Before we can code our app, we need to install Ionic 2. Thankfully it is easy.

Note   If you already have Ionic 1 installed on your machine, you can continue to use it. Installing Ionic 2 will not hinder developing while using Ionic 1.

First, let us install nodejs. Nodejs is a cross-platfrom environment for developing server applications. Don't ask why a server-side environment is needed to install a mobile development framework.

We are going to download and install Nodejs from its web site: `https://nodejs.org/en/download/`. This will also install its package manager npm. After installing nodejs and npm, verify if they are installed properly by issuing the following command at the command line:

```
npm -v
```

© Josephine Eskaline Joyce Justin and Joesph Xavier Judes 2017
J. Justin and J. Jude, *Learn Ionic 2*, https://doi.org/10.1007/978-1-4842-2617-9_2

It should return the version of the npm installed. On my machine, it returns the following:

```
3.10.8
```

Once nodejs and npm are installed, it's time to install Ionic 2. Use the following command to install Ionic 2:

```
npm install -g cordova ionic
```

In some cases, you might need to install using the command (prefixing with sudo)

```
sudo npm install -g cordova ionic
```

As we saw in the first chapter, we need the native software development kits (SDKs) to develop applications for those platforms. iOS applications can be developed only on a Mac; however, Android applications can be developed on any platform. When you install Xcode, iOS SDKs are already installed. Installing Android SDK is complicated. You can find a guide to install Android SDK at `http://ionicframework.com/docs/ionic-cli-faq/#android-sdk`.

If all of these steps go well, you should have Ionic installed on your machine. Go into the terminal, and issue the following command to verify if Ionic is installed properly:

```
ionic -v
```

If this returned without any error, that means you are good to go for the rest of this chapter.

Quick-Start with Ionic Templates

Ionic provides an easy approach to quick-start an app development. It provides a few default templates to create the app. These templates, based on the template selected, come with the default code. Before we start, let's understand these templates. Table 2-1 lists the templates available in Ionic 2 (this list can be seen by issuing the command "ionic start –list" in a terminal).

Table 2-1. *Ionic Templates*

Template name	Purpose	Command to create the project
blank	A blank starter project for Ionic	ionic start MyApp blank --v2
complex-list	A complex list starter template	ionic start MyApp complex-list --v2
maps	An Ionic starter project using Google Maps and a side menu	ionic start MyApp maps --v2
salesforce	A starter project for Ionic and Salesforce	ionic start MyApp salesforce --v2
sidemenu	A starting project for Ionic using a side menu with navigation in the content area	ionic start MyApp sidemenu --v2
tabs	A starting project for Ionic using a simple tabbed interface	ionic start MyApp tabs --v2

Building the App

Coming back to our app development, let's use the "blank" app template to understand the complete details of the app development. Issue the command to create a blank app in a terminal with name of the app as CounterApp.

```
$ ionic start CounterApp blank --v2 --ts
```

In the foregoing command "--v2" instructs Ionic start to build an Ionic 2 app, and "--ts" instructs it to create the app based on TypeScript (We will cover TypeScript in the next chapter).

Now the blank template of the CounterApp is ready. The previous command would create a new folder with the name of the app, CounterApp, in our case, and the project artifacts are placed. Before adding new code or updating any existing code, it's important to understand what this template is creating. To understand it, first let's run the app.

In the same terminal as above, change the directory to the app and let's issue the command "*ionic serve*." Ionic serve command has multiple options which we will discuss in detail later. For now let's run without any options.

Since the app template that we choose is a blank one, Figure 2-1 shows the minimal content in the launched browser.

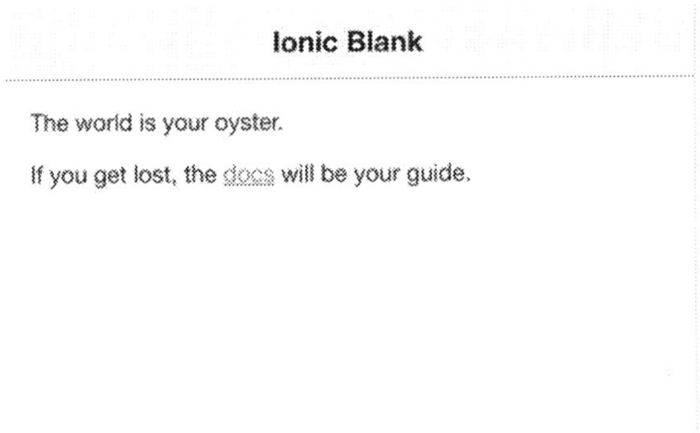

Ionic Blank

The world is your oyster.

If you get lost, the docs will be your guide.

Figure 2-1. *Blank template view of Ionic 2*

Do you want to know how your app will look in various Oss? Open `http://localhost:8100/ionic-lab`, in a browser. Select the platforms to view from the Platforms list.

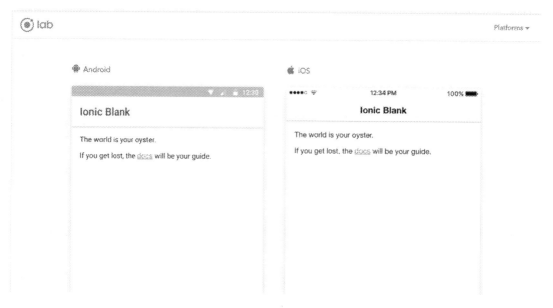

Figure 2-2. *"ionic-lab" view of the blank app*

Folder Structure

Before we understand the generated code, let's review the folder structure of the app as shown in Figure 2-3.

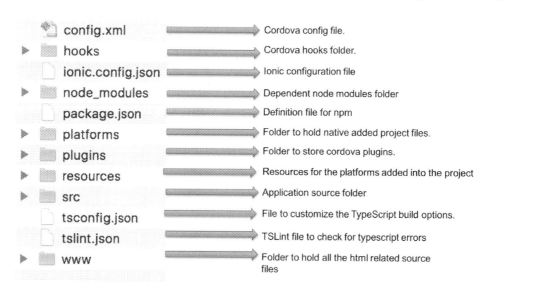

Figure 2-3. *Ionic 2 folder structure*

Ionic 2 organizes the folder structure by feature. All of the logic, templates, and styling of a feature or functionality are kept in the src folder. Figure 2-4 shows the contents of the src folder.

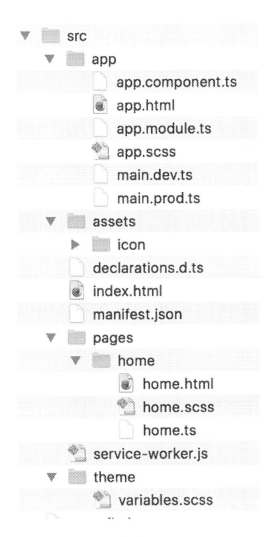

Figure 2-4. *Ionic 2 src folder structure*

index.html is the file which is used to load the entire app. This would be copied to www folder during the app build process. service-worker.js enables offline capabilities when it comes to web apps. To learn more about service workers, refer to https://developer.mozilla.org/en/docs/Web/API/Service_Worker_ API. declaration.d.ts is a definition file which lists the libraries used. theme\variables.scss helps in defining the styling variables.

The src/app folder contains the app level files, and defines how the whole app is compiled and bundled. Following are the details of the files in the app folder:

- app.module.ts–Represents the app as a module.

- app.component.ts–Root component of the app

- app.html–Root view of the app

- app.scss–App style definition

- main.dev.ts / main.prod.ts–Used for bootstrapping the application.

9

Depending on the type of build, one of these files will be used.

In the blank app we created, there is only one functionality to display the blank page, and there is only one folder under app\pages folder, in our case "home" (see Figure 2-4).

Following are the details of the files in the home folder:

- home.html–Template of the page

- home.ts—TypeScript of the page view. This is where the @Component decorator is defined

- home.scss–File that would contain the custom SASS (Syntactically Awesome Style Sheets) for this page. If you are new to SASS refer to http://sass-lang.com/.

To apply styles or themes to Ionic 2 applications, you must modify the html and scss files. .css files are generated from the .scss files.

The www folder is the web root folder of the Ionic app. The build folder under the www folder contains the compiled code of the Ionic 2 applications. In general, there is no need to modify the code inside this folder. index.html in the www folder shows the initial view of the application.

Reviewing the Code

Listing 2-1 contains www/index.html code, which provides a view of the application.

Listing 2-1. www/index.html Code

```
<body>

  <!-- Ionic's root component and where the app will load -->
  <ion-app></ion-app>

  <!-- The polyfills js is generated during the build process -->
  <script src="build/polyfills.js"></script>

  <!-- The bundle js is generated during the build process -->
  <script src="build/main.js"></script>

</body>
```

is the directive that informs Ionic that this is where the CounterApp lives.

Src/app/app.module.ts indicates the HomePage component as the root page of the app. This is the first component to be invoked in the ionic application execution and it controls the rest of the application flow. src/pages/home/home.ts contains the HomePage component of our app (Listing 2-2).

Listing 2-2. src/pages/home/home.ts Code

```
import { Component } from '@angular/core';

import { NavController } from 'ionic-angular';

@Component({
  selector: 'page-home',
  templateUrl: 'home.html'
})
```

```
export class HomePage {

  constructor(public navCtrl: NavController) {

  }

}
```

export class HomePage{} is the root component of our app. We can use this to load other components, if they exist. @Component is a decorator which allows us to add the metadata to our component. In our app, it defines the template associated with.

NavController stores and controls the navigation items in Ionic. Navigation stack contains all the views that you have used previously in the app. You can imagine this as an array of items. To add a view to the stack we use the push method; to remove the view from the stack we use the pop method.

Listing 2-3 contains src/pages/home/home.html, which is the template of our component and contains the Ionic tags to display our view.

Listing 2-3. pages/home/home.html Code

```
<ion-header>
  <ion-navbar>
    <ion-title>
      Ionic Blank
    </ion-title>
  </ion-navbar>
</ion-header>

<ion-content padding>
  The world is your oyster.
  <p>
    If you get lost, the <a href="http://ionicframework.com/docs/v2">docs</a> will be your
guide.
  </p>
</ion-content>
```

creates the top bar displayed in the app. defines the content area of the app. To know more, refer to http://ionicframework.com/docs/api/directive/ionContent/.

Adding Functionality

Now that we understand the folder structure and the files' definitions, let's start to build our CounterApp. A simple process will help us increment a counter or reset it. There are three components in this CounterApp.

- A variable value in the page with the default value as 0.

- A button which, when clicked, should increment the counter variable.

- A button which, when clicked, should reset the counter to its default value.

As our first Ionic 2 app is also a simple one, we will not add a service separately. Instead, we will execute it all together. Later in this book, we will introduce controllers and services.

To display a variable, we need to define it by modifying the HomePage class in the src/pages/home/home.ts file. Let's assign its default value as 0, as shown in Listing 2-4.

Listing 2-4. Changes to the home.ts Code

```
@Component({
  selector: 'page-home',
  templateUrl: 'home.html'
})
export class HomePage {
  public tapCounter: number = 0;
  constructor(public navCtrl: NavController) {
  }
}
```

Now let's look at the code to display this variable's value in the page. Open the `src/pages/home/home.html` file. Modify the title of the page from ***Ionic Blank*** to ***Tap Me*** (Listing 2-5).

Listing 2-5. Changes to the home.html Code

```
<ion-navbar>
    <ion-title>
      Tap Me
    </ion-title>
  </ion-navbar>
```

In Listing 2-6 we add the `<div>` code to the `<ion-content/>`, which would display the variable.

Listing 2-6. Changes to the home.html Code to Display the Variable

```
<ion-content padding>
  <div>
        <p align="center">{{tapCounter}}</p>
  </div>
</ion-content>
```

Now the app would display the title and the counter variable value according to our changes (Figure 2-5). If you are already running ionic serve, refreshing the page should display the new changes.

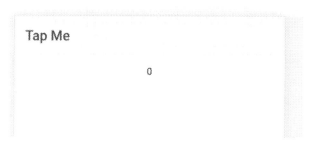

Figure 2-5. *Counter app displaying the variable*

Now let's add buttons to manage the value of this variable and their corresponding methods. Add the buttons into the home.html file, as shown in Listing 2-7.

Listing 2-7. Code to Add the Buttons

```
<ion-content padding>
  <div>
       <p align="center">{{tapCounter}}</p>
  </div>
  <ion-buttons>
    <button ion-button block (click)="buttonTapped()">Tap me!</button>
    <button ion-button block (click)="reset()">Reset</button>
  </ion-buttons>
</ion-content>
```

Clicking these buttons calls two different methods. The buttonTapped method increments the tapCounter variable and the reset method sets the value of the tapCounter to 0. Let's add those two methods in to the home.ts file (Listing 2-8).

Listing 2-8. Code to Add Functionality to Buttons

```
export class HomePage {
       public tapCounter: number = 0;
  constructor(public navCtrl: NavController) {
  }
  buttonTapped() {
       this.tapCounter++;
  }
  reset() {
       this.tapCounter = 0;
  }
}
```

With all the foregoing changes, the app would look like Figure 2-6.

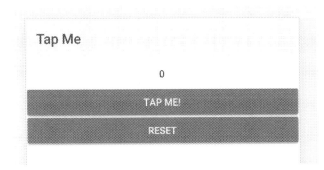

Figure 2-6. *Fully functional CounterApp*

Clicking the Tap Me button would call the method buttonTapped which increments the count of the variable. Clicking the Reset button would call the method reset, which will reset the count variable to 0.

MODIFY THE APP TO INCREASE / DECREASE COUNTER

You can modify the app to include Increase and Decrease buttons in place of the Tap Me! button and include the feature accordingly.

- The Increase button should increase the counter

- The Decrease button should decrease the counter

- The Reset button, which already exists, should reset the counter to 0.

Summary

In this chapter we installed Ionic and learned about the different templates Ionic provides so that we could accelerate our development. We created a CounterApp with the Ionic blank template. We modified the home.html file to add two buttons and displayed value stored in a variable. We also modified the home.ts file to add the functionality of the buttons: when clicked, one button increments the variable value and the other resets the value to 0.

CHAPTER 3

Building Blocks of Ionic

We built our first Ionic app in the previous chapter. Before we dive deep into Ionic components, we need to understand the basic building blocks of Ionic.

Ionic 2 is built on Angular 2, and Angular 2 is built on TypeScript. It is essential to understand these two building blocks if we are to master Ionic 2.

Learning Objectives

- Review TypeScript, a language used by Ionic 2
- Review AngularJS, the JavaScript framework used by Ionic 2

Introduction to TypeScript

TypeScript is superset of JavaScript created by Microsoft. TypeScript brings optional static typing, classes, and interfaces to JavaScript.

This section provides a comprehensive introduction to TypeScript, so we discuss some of the elements of JavaScript here as well.

Comments

TypeScript supports both single line and multiline comments.

```
// this is a single line comment
/* this is a multi line comment.
Multiline comments starts with slash-star and ends with star-slash */
```

Declaration

In TypeScript you use const to declare a constant and let to declare a variable.

```
let  name = "TypeScript";
name = "nodejs";
const pi = 3.141;
```

TypeScript infers type from declaration. In the foregoing example, name is a variable and pi is a constant. Once an identifier has a type, that type can't be changed.

© Josephine Eskaline Joyce Justin and Joesph Xavier Judes 2017
J. Justin and J. Jude, *Learn Ionic 2*, https://doi.org/10.1007/978-1-4842-2617-9_3

You can also specify the type by writing it after the variable, separated by a colon.

```
let name: string = "TypeScript";
```

Basic Types

TypeScript supports all JavaScript types. In addition, it introduces an enumeration type. This section discusses TypeScript datatypes.

Boolean

Boolean variables can hold either a true or a false value.

```
let isDone: boolean = false;
```

Number

All numbers are floating point values in TypeScript, as in JavaScript. TypeScript supports hexadecimal, decimal, binary, and octal literals.

```
let loc: number = 600;
```

String

You can use both double quotes (") and single quotes (') to surround string data.

```
let name = "typescript";
name = "java";
```

TypeScript supports multiline strings, with backtick(`).

```
let subject: string = `TypeScript is awesome.
Google adapting a language developed at Microsoft, shows how awesome it is.`
```

TypeScript supports _template strings_, which can have embedded expressions. Embedded expressions take the form `${expression}`. Embedded expressions are useful in cases like mail-merge where you invoke a templated string multiple times with different value for embedded expressions.

```
let customerName: string = `Harry`;
let invoiceAmount: number = 1500;
let email: string = `Dear ${customerName},
Invoice for ${invoiceAmount} is enclosed.
Thank you.`
```

Any

When it is impossible to know the type, you can use `any`.

```
let userInput: any;
userInput = "any user input"
userInput = 45.3;
userInput = false;
```

Void

void is absence of type. It is commonly used to indicate that a function does not return a value.

```
function showWarning(): void {
        alert("This is a warning")
}
```

Type Assertions

Sometimes you might want to override the inferred type. Then you can use type assertions. There are two forms of type assertion. One is using angle brackets.

```
let name: any = "Bruce Wills";
let nameLen: number = (<string>name).length;
```

The Second form is using as.

```
let name: any = "Bruce Wills";
let nameLen: number = (name as string).length;
```

Type assertions are different from type casting found in other languages. Casting is a runtime operation, whereas assertion is a compile time operation.

Collections

A Collection is a grouping of multiple elements into a single unit. TypeScript supports two types of collections, array and tuple.

Array

Arrays could be typed or generic.

```
let cities: string[] = ['delhi', 'chennai', 'mumbai'];
let cities: Array<string> = ['delhi', 'chennai', 'mumbai'];
```

Tuple

Tuples are used to group fixed number of elements. Their type does not need to be the same.

```
let yearBorn: [string, number];
yearBorn = ['julia roberts', 1967];
```

Enum

Enum gives friendly names to sets of numeric values.

```
enum Day {Sunday, Monday, Tuesday, Wednesday, Thursday, Friday, Saturday};
let firstDay: Day = Day.Sunday;
```

By default, enums begin numbering their members starting at 0. You can override this manually. In fact, you can set values manually for all elements.

```
enum Day {Sunday = 1, Monday, Tuesday, Wednesday, Thursday, Friday, Saturday};
enum Direction {North = 2, South = 4, East = 6, West = 8};
enum Direction {North = 2, South = 4, East, West}; // East = 5; West = 6
```

Union

Sometimes you want variables to be of multiple types. Say a path variable can be either a single string or an array of strings. Then that variable should be of the union type.

```
let path: string[] | string;
path = ['/home', '/home/dropbox'];
path = '/home';
```

Operators

Operators act on variables and constants, specifiying what is to be done to them.

Arithmetic Operators

The binary arithmetic operators are +, -, *, /, %, ++, --.

```
let a = 5;
let b = 4;
let c = 0;
c = a + b; //c = 9
c = a - b; //c = 1
c = a * b; //c = 20
c = a / b; //c = 1.25
c = a % b; //c = 1
c = a++; //c = 6
c = b--; //c = 3
```

Comparison Operators

The comparison operators are ==, ===, !=, >, <, >=, <=.

== and === are equality comparison operators. == checks equality of value, as in any language; === checks equality of value and type.

```
let a = 5;
let b = 4;
let c = false;
let d = 5;

c = a == b; //c = false
c = a === d; //c = true
c = a != b; //c = true
c = a > b; //c = true
c = a < b; //c = false
c = a >= b; //c = true
c = a <= b; //c = false
```

Logical Operators

The logical operators are &&, ||, and !.

&& is a logical AND operator. If both operands are true, then the condition becomes true.

|| is a logical OR operator. If one of the two operands is true, then the condition becomes true.

! is a logical NOT operator. It reverses the state of the operand.

Assignment Operators

The assignment operators are =, +=, -=, *=, /=, %=

= is a simple assignment operators. Others carry out the operation and then assigns the value.

b += a is equivalent to b = b + a

Control Flow

In this section, we will see decision-making and looping statements.

if …else

The if-else statement is a decision-making statement. The syntax of the statement is as follows:

```
if (boolean-expression) {
      statement1
}
else {
      statement2
}
```

The else part of the statement is optional.

ternary operator

This ternary operator is a simplified, concise if-else statement. It takes the following form:

```
boolean-expression ? statement1 : statement2

let speed = 80;
let isFast = speed > 55 ? true : false
```

Following is a detailed example that allows you to find out if the year is a leap year.

```
let year = 2016

let isLeapYear = ((year % 400) == 0) ? 1 :
                    (((year % 100) == 0)? 0 :
                    (((year % 4) == 0)  ? 1 :
                    0));//default result
alert(isLeapYear)
```

for loop

We use for loop when we know how many times a task has to be repeated.

```
var sum = 0;
for (var i = 0; i <= 1000; i++){
    if (i % 3 == 0 || i % 5 == 0){
        sum = sum + i;
    }
}
console.log(sum);
```

for-of loop

TypeScript introduces a `for-of` loop (since TypeScript is a superset, you can also use the existing for-in loop) to loop through collections.

```
let cities: string[] = ['delhi', 'chennai', 'mumbai'];

for (let city of cities) {
        alert(city);
}
```

switch

The switch statement is an enhanced `if-else` statement, which is convenient to use if there are many options to choose.

```
let animal = 'dog';

switch (animal){
        case 'dog':
                alert('dog');
                break;
        case 'cat':
                alert('cat');
                break;
        default:
                alert('none?')
}
```

while

Use while to execute a task until a given condition is true.

```
let sum = 0;
while (sum <= 5) {
        sum = sum + 1;
}
```

do...while

do...while is similar to the `while` loop, except that the statement is guaranteed to run at least once.

```
let sum = 0;
do {
        sum = sum + 1;
} while (sum <= 4)
```

Functions

In TypeScript you declare functions similar to JavaScript, with type information.

```
function squareOf(i: number): number {
        return i * i;
};
```

You can interfere with return types, so we can declare a function as follows:

```
function squareOf(i: number) { return i * i };
```

In TypeScript, as in JavaScript, functions are first-class citizens. This means we can assign functions to variables and pass functions as parameters. We can also write anonymous functions. All of the following will generate the same JavaScript:

```
let sqr1 = function sqr (i: number) : number {
        return i * i;
}
```

```
// anonymous function
let sqr2 = function (i: number) : number {
        return i * i;
}

// alternate syntax for anonymous function using =>
let sqr3 = (i: number) : number => { return i * i;}

// return type can be inferred
let sqr4 = (i: number)  => { return i * i;}

// return is optional in one line functions
let sqr5 = (i: number) => i * i
```

Optional and Default Values

Functions can take optional values. You mention the optional values by using ?: syntax.

```
function getFullName(firstName: string, lastName?: string) : string {
        if (lastName) {
                return firstName + " " + lastName;
        } else {
                return firstName
        }
}
```

You can also mention default values for parameters.

```
function getFullName(firstName: string, lastName: string = "") : string {
        return (firstName + " " + lastName).trim();
}
```

Classes

TypeScript brings object-oriented approach to JavaScript. Let us consider an example.

Say you are developing a digital library of books. Then you can define a Book class as follows:

```
class Book {
        name: string;
        purchasedYear: number;

        constructor (name: string, purchasedYear: number){
                this.name = name;
                this.purchasedYear = purchasedYear;
        }
}

let Book1 = new Book('7 habits', 2005)
```

TypeScript also supports subclassing or inheritance. If you want to extend the digital library to include all assets like CDs, PDFs, and so on, you can modify the above class into a superclass and many subclasses.

```
class Asset {
        name: string;
        purchasedYear: number;

        constructor (name: string, purchasedYear: number){
                this.name = name;
                this.purchasedYear = purchasedYear;
        }
}

class Book extends Asset {
        constructor (name: string, purchasedYear: number) {
                super(name, purchasedYear)
        }
}
let book1 = new Book('7-habits', 2013);
```

Interfaces

Interfaces allow multiple objects to expose **common** functionality. By using an interface, you can ensure that all these assets implement a common functionality (e.g., name, purchased year, and age). Interface is only a contract; implementation is carried out at the class level.

```
interface iAsset {
        name: string;
        purchasedYear: number;
        age: () => number;
}

class Book implements iAsset{
        name: string;
        purchasedYear: number;

        constructor (name: string, purchasedYear: number){
                this.name = name;
                this.purchasedYear = purchasedYear;
        }
        age() {
                return (2016 - this.purchasedYear);
        }

}

let Book1 = new Book('7 habits', 2005)
alert(Book1.age)
```

Introduction to AngularJS 2

AngularJS is a client-side JavaScript framework to create web applications. It enhances HTML to describe user interface and behavior by way of directives; it enables building data-driven applications with its two-way data binding approach.

Let us look at each of these elements in detail.

Module

Like any modern development system, AngularJS is modular. An AngularJS application, and hence an Ionic application, is composed of many existing modules.

Almost all of the AngularJS application have to create a component. This is a library module and you import it as follows:

```
import { Component } from '@angular2/core';
```

You can also divide your code into logical units, such as modules. This increases the reusability of your code. You create a module by exporting a class in your file. You import your modules using a relative path as follows:

```
import {HomePage} from '../home/home';
```

Directives

Directives are the fundamental building blocks of AngularJS. They either modify the layout structure or modify aspects of DOM (Document Object Model) elements. There are three types of directives: structural directives, attribute directives, and components.

▓ **Note**   AngularJS comes with few built-in directives and you can also define your own directives.

Structural Directives

Structural directives alter the layout by adding or removing DOM elements.

- *ngFor: `*ngFor` is a repeat directive. It repeats a template once per item in a collection. For example, see

  ```
  <div *ngFor="let item of items"></div>
  ```

  This will create one `<div>` element for each `item` in the `items` collection.

- *ngIf: *ngIf adds or removes an element and its children to the DOM based on a condition.

  ```
  <item-detail *ngIf="atruestmt"></item-detail>
  ```

This will display this item only if `atruestmt` evaluates to true.

- ngSwitch: Use ngSwitch when you want to display different elements depending on a condition.

```
<span [ngSwitch]="myChoice">
        <span *ngSwitchCase="'A'">You selected A</span>
        <span *ngSwitchCase="'B'">You selected B</span>
        <span *ngSwitchCase="'C'">You selected C</span>
        <span ngSwitchDefault>You selected none</span>
</span>
```

Attribute Directives

Attribute directives attach behavior or alter the appearance of a particular element.

- ngClass
- ngStyle
- ngModel

Component

Components are special directives and are associated with a view. They are decorated with `` `@Component` `` decorator.

Component is a class decorator that represents a UI element on the screen with its properties and behavior. It is a directive with template.

Let's dig into Component with a helloworld example.

```
import {Component} from 'angular2/core;

@Component ({
        selector: 'helloworld';
        template: `<div>Hello World!</div>;
})

class HelloWorld{}
```

This component introduces a UI element, in this case an HTML tag, helloworld, with a template `<div>Hello World!</div>`.

It can be used in HTML as follows:

```
<body>
        <helloworld></helloworld>
</body>
```

Metadata

In the aforementioned example, selector and template are metadata that define the look and behavior of this component. Almost all components will contain these two metadata. There are other metadata fields like templateUrl, directives, and providers.

Template

A component's view is defined by templates. Like any templating engine, AngularJS extends HTML and adds its own elements and attributes. AngularJS elements are primarily for data binding. Using data binding, we can display data from application, as well as updating the application from data provided by the user.

Interpolation

Interpolation is the first form of the data binding. Interpolation is displaying the value of a component property in HTML. It goes as follows:

```
<div>My Name is {{name}}</div>
```

Here, AngularJS will replace name with the string value of the corresponding property.

Binding Properties

We can initialize and update the property of an element through template expressions.

```
<span [id]="postId">
```

Here the id of this span element will be set to the value of postId. If and when the value of postId changes, the id will get changed as well.

This is one-way data binding, as the data flows in only one direction—from the expression to the target—which is property of the element. You can use interpolation most of the scenarios than property binding.

Binding Events

You can configure your application to listen to events like keystrokes and clicks by binding events. This is still one-way data binding as data flows from the elements to target method.

```
<button (click)="onSave()">Save</button>
```

Here, with one click of the button, onSave() method is invoked.

Two-Way Binding

If you want to display a property value as well as update that property when the user changes the value, you use two-way binding.

```
<input [(ngModel)]="postTitle">
```

Services

Services are classes that encapsulate data and function to offer a feature. Angular doesn't mandate any specification for service. Yet, you will find services everywhere.

```
export class Logger {
  log(msg: any)   { console.log(msg); }
}

export class GeneratePostsService{
  constructor(
    private logger: Logger) {
        this.logger.log('creating posts');
    }

  }
```

Though you could write the entire business logic within the component, it is a recommended practice to keep the component lean and delegate all business logic to services.

Summary

We learned the basics of TypeScript and AngularJS. TypeScript introduces static typing, an object-oriented approach to JavaScript. AngularJS is a JavaScript framework for creating web applications.

In the subsequent chapters we will see how Ionic uses these two technologies to build mobile applications.

CHAPTER 4

Those Famous Quotes

Use the HTTP REST call to read a json file and display the list/details view. Quickly check the behavior of the app in the browser and run the app on different mobile platforms. Use a social sharing plug-in with the app to share on twitter using the twitter app available in the device.

Learning Objectives

- Use HTTP to retrieve data
- Use a multipage app in Ionic 2
- Display list
- Navigate between pages in an app and pass information
- Install Cordova plug-in on an app
- Share on twitter
- Add mobile platforms to the app
- Run the app in Android/iOS platforms

What We Will build

We are going to build a "Those Famous Quotes" app, which allows us to search famous quotes by author name. Once the search results are displayed, you can select a quote to view its complete details. Quote search results are displayed on one page and the details are displayed on another page. We use item click to navigate from the list to the details page, and we use a back button to navigate from the details page to the list/search page.

Ionic Generate

Ionic CLI (command-line interface) provides an "ionic generate" feature. This feature helps to easily move from a basic app to a full-featured app. This tool saves us a lot of work in generating the required app artifacts. It also helps to keep the structure of the app under control. You can see a list of available generators (as shown in Figure 4-1) by using the "ionic generate --list" command.

```
$ ionic generate --list
Available generators:
 * Component
 * Directive
 * Page
 * Pipe
 * Provider
 * Tabs
```

Figure 4-1. *List of available generators*

In this chapter we will use the generator to create pages. And we will use this "ionic generate" tool to create other components of Ionic 2 in the upcoming chapters.

Let's Build the App

To build this app, let's begin with the blank template and use ionic-cli to generate pages—list and details view. We include a search feature on the page, to filter the data. The details view allows the user to share the quotes on twitter. We can also run the app in a device to see how it works on various platform devices.

As we did in our last chapter, let's use the "blank" app template to create the basic app template. Issue the command to create a blank app in a terminal (as shown in Listing 4-1). The name of the app is QuotesApp.

Listing 4-1. Blank App Creation

```
$ ionic start QuotesApp blank --v2 --ts
```

Now the blank template of the QuotesApp is ready. Before we add any features to this app, let's create the two pages necessary for listing quotes and displaying quote details.

Add Pages

To add a page, run the command "ionic generate page <name>" as shown in Listing 4-2. This should be run within the folder of the app. So change the directory to "QuotesApp" created in the above step.

Listing 4-2. Generate Page

```
$ ionic generate page quotes-list --ts
```

"--ts" in the command indicates that the created page artifacts should be based on the typescript. Since this is a page creation, three files are added. In the previous chapter, the home page had an html file, a ts file, and a scss file. Those three files are created for the page name that we defined in the command.

Similarly, create the quotes-detail page using the command "ionic generate page quotes-detail --ts."

To refer the newly created pages in the root component of the app, modify the `src/app/app.component.ts` file, as shown in the Listing 4-3. Also modify the rootPage as the quotes-list page.

Listing 4-3. src/app/app.component.ts Code

```
import { QuotesListPage } from '../pages/quotes-list/quotes-list';

@Component({
  templateUrl: 'app.html'
})
export class MyApp {
  rootPage = QuotesListPage;
```

To list the new pages as the modules of the app, modify the `src/app/app.module.ts` file (Listing 4-4).

Listing 4-4. src/app/app.module.ts Code

```
import { QuotesListPage } from '../pages/quotes-list/quotes-list';
import { QuotesDetailPage } from '../pages/quotes-detail/quotes-detail';

@NgModule({
  declarations: [
    MyApp,
    QuotesListPage,
    QuotesDetailPage
  ],
  imports: [
    IonicModule.forRoot(MyApp)
  ],
  bootstrap: [IonicApp],
  entryComponents: [
    MyApp,
    QuotesListPage,
    QuotesDetailPage
  ],
  providers: [{provide: ErrorHandler, useClass: IonicErrorHandler}]
})
```

Open the `src/pages/quotes-list/quotes-list.ts` file. This file contains the generated class for the page QuotesListPage. Similarly open the `pages/quotes-list/quotes-detail.ts` file. This file contains the generated class for the page QuotesDetailPage. These two pages are not linked together, which we will do in this chapter.

Ionic's blank template creates a home page in the app. We will not be using that for this app. So delete the "import { HomePage } from '../pages/home/home'; "from app.module.ts & app.component.ts file and also delete the `src/pages/home` folder.

Making a REST HTTP Request

In this chapter we will just use a basic REST HTTP call. This app reads a json file which contains all the quotes and its details. A HTTP call is used to retrieve the json file content and loads the json to a local variable. We need the http objects to be available to the `quotes-list.ts` file.

To import the necessary components, add the code in Listing 4-5 to the top of the file.

Listing 4-5. src/pages/quotes-list/quotes-list.ts Imports Code

```
import {Http} from '@angular/http';
import 'rxjs/add/operator/map';
import {QuotesDetailPage} from '../quotes-detail/quotes-detail';
```

- **Http**—Service to handle requests. HTTP calls returns observable of HTTP Responses (Observable<Response>). Observables are Angular 2 concepts which are similar to Promises. Differing from Promises, observables can return multiple values over time. Observables can be treated as arrays. This allows the usage of methods like map and flatmap, to reduce the observable returns.

- **RxJS Library**—Reactive Extensions Library for JavaScript. This is a library for composing asynchronous and event-based programs using observables. We are including the map operator in our class, which we will use to manage the JSON return. This is used to transform the return object of collection.

- **QuotesDetailPage**—Including the class for navigating to the details page.

Update the constructor of the quotes-list to make the http call (see Listing 4-6).

Listing 4-6. pages/quotes-list/quotes-list.ts Constructor Code

```
quotesList = [];
filteredQuotes = [];
isfiltered: boolean ;

  constructor(private http:Http, private navController: NavController) {
    this.isfiltered = false;
    this.http.get('quotes.json')
    .map(res => res.json())
    .subscribe(
        data => {
          this.quotesList = data.quotes;
        },
        err => console.log("error is "+err), // error
        () => console.log('read quotes Complete '+ this.quotesList) // complete
    );

  }
```

quotesList is the variable defined to contain the json object. filteredQuotes is the variable which will contain the search results. Constructor is modified to inject the Http object, which will be used to make the http call. The HTTP get call takes a URL (uniform resource locator). In our case we want to load the JSON, so we can do this in two ways. We can either provide the URL of the JSON or copy the json file into the app's www folder and provide the file name instead of the complete URL. You can download the json file from http://www.apress.com/9781484226162.

map is an operator used to transform the result to the object of the type that we need. In our case we want a JSON object. So we are transforming the res object to res.json(). Operator subscribe helps us to subscribe to the observable. The format for subscribe is "subscribe(success, failure, complete)." In our case, for the success we assign the return to the quotesList variable.

Search Feature

QuotesApp allows searching through the quotes list with the author name. HTML needs to be added to the quotes-list.html to display the search bar and the quotes results. Add the code in Listing 4-7, to the <ion-content> in the quotes-list.html file in the /pages/quotes-list folder.

Listing 4-7. src/pages/quotes-list/quotes-list.html Code

```
<ion-input type="text" placeholder="Search Quotes..." (input)="searchQuotes($event)">
</ion-input>
        </ion-item>

        <ion-list *ngIf="!isfiltered">
                <ion-item *ngFor="let quote1 of quotesList" (click)="itemTapped($event,
                quote1)">
                        <h2>{{quote1.author}}</h2>
                        <p class="item-description">{{quote1.quote}}</p>
                </ion-item>
        </ion-list>

        <ion-list *ngIf="isfiltered">
                <ion-item *ngFor="let quote of filteredQuotes" (click)="itemTapped($event,
                quote)">
                        <h2>{{quote.author}}</h2>
                        <p class="item-description">{{quote.quote}}</p>
                </ion-item>
        </ion-list>
```

The first ion-list is displayed when the isfiltered value is false, to display the entire list of quotes. The second ion-list is displayed when the isfiltered value is true, to display only the filtered list of quotes.

searchQuotes() is called for searching the json object. searchQuotes is a method in the quotes-list.ts file and contains the code in Listing 4-8. This code just gets the value typed in the search box, and if it's more than two characters, it will filter the quotes from the quotesList variable. Based on the search key, the filtered list will be copied into the filteredQuotes variable.

Listing 4-8. pages/quotes-list/quotes-list.ts searchQuotes Code

```
searchQuotes(event) {
            if(event.target.value.length > 2) {
    var filteredJson = this.quotesList.filter(function (row) {
      if(row.author.indexOf(event.target.value) != -1) {
        return true
      } else {
        return false;
      }
    });
    this.isfiltered = true;
    this.filteredQuotes = filteredJson;
            }
    }
```

Modify the quotes-list page title to "Quotes List" by modifying the ion-title (Listing 4-9).

Listing 4-9. pages/quotes-list/quotes-list.html Title Change Code

```
<ion-navbar>
    <ion-title>Quotes List</ion-title>
</ion-navbar>
```

Let's run the app to verify if the search works as expected. In the command line issue the command **ionic serve** to run the app. The browser should be launched to display the app as shown in Figure 4-2.

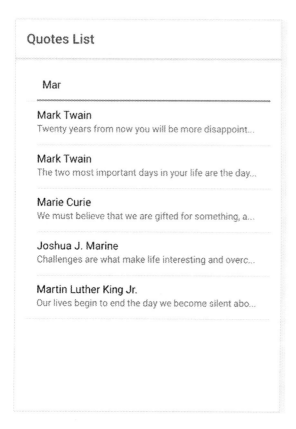

Figure 4-2. Search results page view

At this point, clicking the item would lead to an error thrown in the console. This is because the tapping of the item has not been completely implemented. It is being done in the following section.

Ionic Navigation

Before we add navigation to the details page, let's come to an understanding of navigation in ionic.

Navigation Stack

Like the browser history, each time you visit a page in an Ionic app, it gets added to the stack as a navigation stack. Each item in the stack has been viewed previously.

A navigation stack is stored in and controlled by NavController in Ionic. To manipulate the stack, we inject the NavController class to a @Page. "Push" is a method by which we add items to the stack and "pop" is a method to remove the items from the stack. While navigating from one page to another we push the page into the stack and to go back to the already viewed page we pop the view off.

NavController

NavController is used to control the navigation of the app. To navigate through an app, create and navigate through a NavController using the `ion-nav` component.

```
@Component(
    template: `<ion-nav [root]="rootPage"></ion-nav>`
})
```

NavController is injected into the constructor. This helps in getting a reference to the NavController to control the navigation of the app. `push()` and `pop()` methods can be used to add and remove views.

```
import { NavController } from 'ionic-angular';
constructor(private navCtrl: NavController) {
  }
```

Passing Data Between Pages

NavParams are objects that exist on a page and contain the data for that particular view.

```
constructor(public params: NavParams){
    // userParams is an object we have in our nav-parameters
    this.params.get('userParams');
  }
```

Add Page Navigation to the QuotesApp

Now that we have the Quotes listing view, let's add the details view. When an item in the search result is clicked, details of the quotes should be displayed. In our app, list page displays the quote only partially, but the details will display the entire quote. However, more details can be displayed in the Details page, if there are any.

First, to capture the item being tapped in the list view, include the following method in the `quotes-list.ts` file (Listing 4-10). This is called from the `quotes-list.html` file when the item is tapped and the tapped quote is passed.

Listing 4-10. page/quotes-list/quotes-list.ts itemTapped Code

```
itemTapped(event, quote) {
            console.log(quote);
            this.navController.push(QuotesDetailPage, {
                    quote: quote
            });
    }
```

The itemTapped method performs two actions. One is to navigate to QuotesDetailPage by adding the QuotesDetailPage to the app navigation and second is to pass the quote that is selected as a NavParam.

Modify the constructor of the QuotesDetailPage in the pages/quotes-detail/quotes-detail.ts file as shown in Listing 4-11. This retrieves the selected quote from the NavParams and assigns it to the variable which is used to display the details of the Quote.

Listing 4-11. page/quotes-detail/quotes-detail.ts Constructor Code

```
quoteDetail: {quote:'', author:''};

  constructor(private navCtrl: NavController,private navParams: NavParams) {
    this.quoteDetail = navParams.get('quote');

  }
```

Now to display the quotes details modify the pages/quotes-detail/quotes-detail.html ion-content with the variable which is populated with the quote details (Listing 4-12).

Listing 4-12. page/quotes-detail/quotes-detail.html Code

```
<ion-content padding>
<h5>{{quoteDetail.quote}}</h5>
<h3> -  {{quoteDetail.author}}</h3>
</ion-content>
```

Modify the quotes-detail page title to "Quotes Details" by modifying the ion-title (Listing 4-13).

Listing 4-13. pages/quotes-list/quotes-list.html Title Change Code

```
<ion-navbar>
    <ion-title>Quotes Detail</ion-title>
  </ion-navbar>
```

Run the app using "ionic serve"; tapping the quote item will display the new details page. Since the navigation of the app contains two pages, going back to the list page from the details page is automatically enabled by Ionic as shown in Figure 4-3.

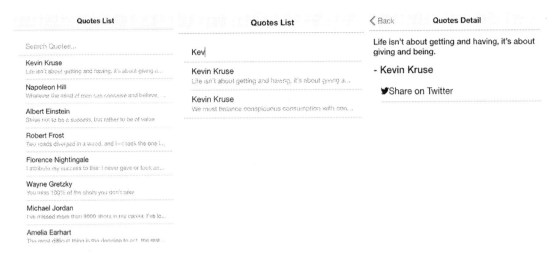

Figure 4-3. *App list and details view*

Just to recap on what we did, we created a Quotes app with the Ionic blank template. We added two pages with the ionic generate CLI. Then we added the http call to retrieve required data. We also added the page navigation between two pages and passed parameters between the pages.

Share on Twitter

The social sharing plug-in needs to be installed for the app to use sharing on Twitter. To install the plug-in, issue the ionic plug-in add command as shown in the Listing 4-14.

Listing 4-14. Social Sharing Plug-in Addition

```
$ ionic plugin add cordova-plugin-x-socialsharing
```

To share the quote to the Twitter account, add the sharing icon to the `quotes-detail.html` file before the `</ion-content>` (Listing 4-15). Ionic provides icons which can be used. For the complete list of icons, visit `http://ionicons.com/`.

Listing 4-15. page/quotes-detail/quotes-detail.html Code for Twitter Share

```
<ion-item (click)="twitterShare()">
  <ion-icon name="logo-twitter">Share on Twitter</ion-icon>
</ion-item>
```

Twitter share needs the social sharing plug-in to be added to the app. Add the code shown in Listing 4-16 to the `quotest-detail.ts` file.

Listing 4-16. Adding SocialSharing Plug-in

```
import { SocialSharing } from 'ionic-native';
```

Add the `twitterShare()` method to the `QuotesDetailPage` class in the `quotes-detail.ts` file as shown in Listing 4-17. The SocialSharing plug-in is from the ionic-native module and will work only when run inside a device or simulator. When you click the share icon from a browser you will notice an error thrown.

Listing 4-17. page/quotes-detail/quotes-detail.ts Code for Twitter Share

```
twitterShare(){
    console.log("in twitter share");
    let quote: string = this.quoteDetail.quote;
    SocialSharing.shareViaTwitter(quote.substring(0,110)+"..",null /*Image*/,"http://
ionicframework.com/img/homepage/ionicview-icon_2x.png")
    .then((data )=>{
        alert("Success "+data);
    },

    (err)=>{
        alert("failed "+err)
    })
}
```

Just to recap what we did, we have two pages on the app. These pages were added using the ionic-cli. Quotes List page displays the list of quotes read from a json file. A filter is applied to the list if a search string is typed. When you click an item in the list, the Quotes Detail page is displayed with only the details of the selected quotes. Also a Twitter share icon is displayed which allows the user to share the quote if the app is viewed in the simulator or device.

Running the App

Until now, we were running the app in a browser. To run the app in an emulator or a device we need to add the appropriate platforms. The following steps help in understanding how this app can be run on Android or iOS platforms.

Add Platforms

To add the respective platforms, run the "ionic platform" command with the platforms that are to be added for the app. Similar to Listing 4-18, issue ionic platform add windows. iOS platform is added into the Ionic app by default.

Listing 4-18. Android Platform Addition

```
$ ionic platform add android
```

Build the App

To build the app, the "ionic build" command is used as shown in Listing 4-19. Similarly, you can build the app in other environments too, like "ionic build ios."

Listing 4-19. Android Platform Build

```
$ ionic build android
```

Running the App in Android

You need to have the Android SDK installed on the machine to run your app. To run the app for android platform, you can choose to run it on a real android device or an emulator.

If the Android SDK is installed and device images are defined in the avd manager, then to emulate your app you can just use ionic emulate as shown in Listing 4-20.

Listing 4-20. Android app on the emulator

```
$ ionic emulate android
```

This would launch the emulator and display the app. If you don't have the emualator images defined, you will receive an error "*Error: No emulator images (avds) found."*

To deploy the app on a real device, you can use the ionic run command (Listing 4-21). This would deploy the app to a real device if available; otherwise it will deploy it to an emulator.

Listing 4-21. Android Platform Run

```
$ ionic run android
```

The quotes app would be displayed in the emulator as shown in Figure 4-4.

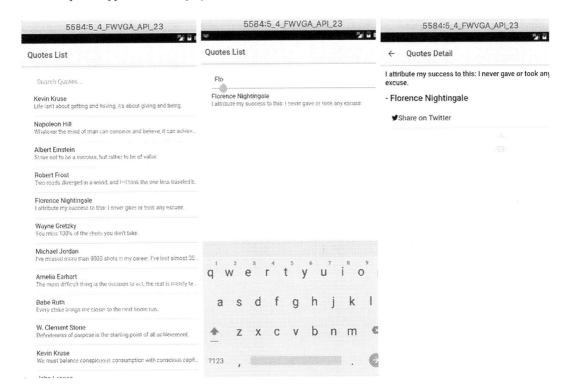

Figure 4-4. *Quotes app on an emulator*

▓ **Note**   If your emulator or device does not have the required app, Twitter in this case, you may not see the sharing icon work as expected.

Running the App in iOS

If you have xcode installed, iOS simulator is available along with it. To run the app for the iOS platform, you can choose to run it on a real Android device or an emulator. To run the app on an emulator, issue the ionic emulate command as shown in Listing 4-22.

Listing 4-22. iOS Platform Emulate

```
$ ionic emulate ios
```

This would launch the emulator and display the app. In the foregoing command, because no target is specified it might choose a default. To list all the possible targets run the command "ionic emulate ios -list." From this list you can choose one of the available emulators as the target as shown in Listing 4-23.

Listing 4-23. iOS Platform Emulate

```
$ ionic emulate ios -target="iPhone-5, 9.3"
```

To deploy the app on a real iOS device, you can use the ionic run command (Listing 4-24).

Listing 4-24. iOS Platform Run

```
$ ionic run ios --device
```

▓ **Note**   If your emulator or device does not have the required app, Twitter in this case, you may not see the sharing icon work as expected.

The quotes app would be displayed in the ios emulator as shown in Figure 4-5.

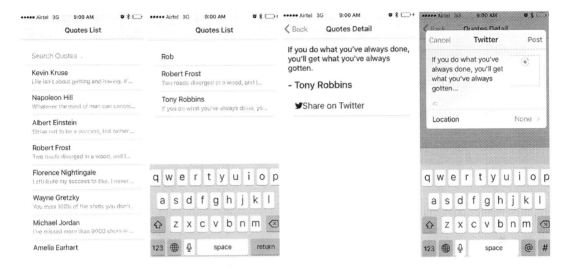

Figure 4-5. *Running the App*

While running the app, if you face *Signing for "QuotesApp" requires a development team.* Then open the platforms/ios/QuotesApp.xcodeproj in a xcode and assign the profile rightly before you run the app.

MODIFY THE APP WITH ADDITIONAL FUNCTIONALITY

You can modify the app to include the following features:

- In the quotes list, modify the filtering not to match the character case of the entered text. This way one should a greater number of results in the quotes list

- Also enable sharing of the quotes in other medium like whatsapp or facebook

Summary

In this chapter, we created a blank app and added two pages to it. Quotes List page displays the list of quotes and when filtered displays the filtered list. This is done by reading a quotes.json file by making an http REST call. When you click an item in the list, the app navigates to the Quotes Detail page with the item details along with a share icon. When clicked, this share icon displays the social sharing plug-in used to launch the Twitter app, if installed in the device. This plug-in allows you ro share the selected quote to the Twitter account configured in the Twitter app.

CHAPTER 5

Build the Weather App

In this chapter you'll retrieve weather data by making an HTTP REST call and taking a closer look at the behavior of forms and form validations. You'll then see how to integrate other modules and display the charts to represent the weather data.

Learning Objectives

- Use HTTP to retrieve data

- Use the tab view

- Forms, Form Fields, Form validations

- Integrate angular modules

- Use charts to display data

What We Will Build

Now it's time to build a "Weather App" that displays the current weather and a weather forecast in two tabs. The user can enter the location in a form, and the app will validate the location and retrieve weather for that location via the `https://developer.forecast.io/` APIs (application programming interfaces). This app also fetches the forecast for the location and displays it in a chart format.

Prerequisite

To use the `https://developer.forecast.io/` APIs you have to register with this site and get the API key. The API key is available from the Ionic Service Providers.

▒ **Note** You can also use any other publicly available APIs to retrieve weather details.

Let's Build the App

Create a blank app named WeatherApp and remove the home page, which is created by default, as we did in the earlier chapters.

For the weather view, we will have two tabs. Issue the `ionic generate tabs WeatherAPI` command and select 2 as the number of tabs (Figure 5-1).

```
$ ionic generate tabs WeatherAPI
? How many tabs would you like?
  1
> 2
  3
  4
  5
```

Figure 5-1. *ionic generate command to create tabs*

Once you have selected the number of tabs, name the first tab "Weather" and the second "Forecast," as shown in Figure 5-2.

```
$ ionic generate tabs WeatherAPI
? How many tabs would you like? 2
? Enter the first tab name: Weather
? Enter the second tab name: Forecast
```

Figure 5-2. *Tabs generation*

Update the `/src/pages/weather-api/weather-api.ts` file with the right import of the pages as shown in Listing 5-1.

Listing 5-1. Tab Import Correction

```
import { WeatherPage } from '../weather/weather'
import { ForecastPage } from '../forecast/forecast'
```

Similarly, update the tab root reference as shown in Listing 5-2.

Listing 5-2. Tab Root Page Upate

```
tab1Root: any = WeatherPage;
tab2Root: any = ForecastPage;
```

To list all pages as the modules of the app, modify `src/app/app.module.ts` file as shown in Listing 5-3. The home page reference can be removed too.

Listing 5-3. Modules Update

```
import { NgModule, ErrorHandler } from '@angular/core';
import { IonicApp, IonicModule, IonicErrorHandler } from 'ionic-angular';
import { MyApp } from './app.component';
import { WeatherAPIPage } from '../pages/weather-api/weather-api';
import { ForecastPage } from '../pages/forecast/forecast';
```

```
import { WeatherPage } from '../pages/weather/weather';

@NgModule({
  declarations: [
    MyApp,
    WeatherAPIPage,
    ForecastPage,
    WeatherPage
  ],
  imports: [
    IonicModule.forRoot(MyApp)
  ],
  bootstrap: [IonicApp],
  entryComponents: [
    MyApp,
    WeatherAPIPage,
    ForecastPage,
    WeatherPage
  ],
  providers: [{provide: ErrorHandler, useClass: IonicErrorHandler}]
})
export class AppModule {}
```

To modify the root page to be the root of the tab, modify the src/app/app.component.ts file as shown in Listing 5-4.

Listing 5-4. Component Root Page Update

```
import { Component } from '@angular/core';
import { Platform } from 'ionic-angular';
import { StatusBar, Splashscreen } from 'ionic-native';
import { WeatherAPIPage } from '../pages/weather-api/weather-api';

@Component({
  templateUrl: 'app.html'
})
export class MyApp {
  rootPage = WeatherAPIPage;

  constructor(platform: Platform) {
    platform.ready().then(() => {
      // Okay, so the platform is ready and our plugins are available.
      // Here you can do any higher level native things you might need.
      StatusBar.styleDefault();
      Splashscreen.hide();
    });
  }
}
```

Adding Data Services

In the weather app, when you provide a location as input, the latitude and longitude of the location are required. You can retrieve this information using the google API. Once you have those details you can retrieve the weather details of the location using the forecast API. We will implement both these calls as services.

An application may use more than few constants. For example, in the WeatherApp, the google API URL (uniform resource locator) and the forecast URL are constants. To avoid hard-coding in multiple places, it's better to bring such hard-coding from one single provider.

Add the Constants Service Provider

Using `ionic` generate create a provider for the constants and name it AppConstants (Listing 5-5).

Listing 5-5. Constants Provider Generation

```
$ ionic generate provider AppConstants
```

The app needs two constants. Add both the constants and their corresponding get methods to this provider. Add the code shown in Listing 5-6 to the AppConstants class by replacing the existing constructor.

Listing 5-6. src/providers/app-constants.js Code

```
googleAPIURL: string;
forecastURL: string;

constructor(private http: Http) {
  this.googleAPIURL = "https://maps.googleapis.com/maps/api/geocode/json?address=";
  this.forecastURL = "https://api.forecast.io/forecast/<<ApiKey of Forecast.io>>/";
}

getGoogleAPIURL() {
  return this.googleAPIURL;
}

getForecastURL() {
  return this.forecastURL;
}
```

In the weather app, we don't set the value of the constants from the app, so we don't have any setter methods included in the provider. But if the app requires calling the setter method, you can added that too.

Add the REST Service Provider

Create the REST service provider with the name WeatherApi (see Listing 5-7).

Listing 5-7. WeatherAPI Provider Creation

```
$ ionic generate provider WeatherAPI
```

The REST provider class needs to use the app-constants provider for the HTTP URL requests. So import app-constants into the WeatherAPI provider file `src/providers/weather-api.ts`, as shown in Listing 5-8.

Listing 5-8. Import app-constants Provider

```
import {AppConstants} from './app-constants';
```

The WeatherAPI constructor should contain two variables: the http object and AppConstants. getGeometry is the method the components can call to retrieve the latitude and longitude for the provided location. This is done by calling the geocode API from google maps. getCurrentWeather is another method that retrieves the weather information for the provided longitude and latitude of the location. Replace the constructor of weather-api.ts file with the code in Listing 5-9.

Listing 5-9. src/providers/weather-api.ts Code

```
  weatherURL: string;
  private constantVar: any;

  constructor(private http: Http, constantVar: AppConstants) {
    this.constantVar = constantVar;
this.weatherURL = constantVar.getForecastURL();
  }

  getCurrentWeather(longitude: any,latitude: any) {
      return this.http.get(this.weatherURL+latitude+","+longitude)
      .map(res => res.json())
  }

    getGeometry(googleAPIURL: any,location: any) {
return this.http.get(googleAPIURL+"'"+location+"'")
      .map(res => res.json())
  }
```

Notice the @Injectable() annotation in the provider classes. This marks the class to be available for the component for instantiation.

Forms in Ionic

Forms can be implemented in three ways in Ionic:

- [(ngModel]
- Forms with Templates
- Forms with FormBuilder

[(ngModel)]

This is a simple API that binds and passes the object to the class. Templates uses ngModels to bind the object and ngSubmit to submit the form. When using ngModel, "name" property is required for the form fields. Listing 5-10 provides an example of how the ngModel is used in forms.

Listing 5-10. ngModel-Based Templates

```
<form (ngSubmit)="loginForm()">
      <ion-item>
```

```
      <ion-label>Login </ion-label>
      <ion-input type="text" [(ngModel)]="login.username" name="username"></ion-input>
    </ion-item>
<button type="submit" block>Login</button>
 </form>
```

Class contains the submit form which can use this.<object> format to retrieve the value as shown in Listing 5-11.

Listing 5-11. ngModel-Based Form Submission

```
login = {}
loginForm () {
    console.log(this. username)
  }
```

Forms with Templates

This way of Form implementation uses the reference to the form instead of the model of the form. The values are pulled directly from the form itself, which is similar to the ngModel way of implementation. The main difference is that the ngModel uses the model of the form, but the template uses the form reference itself (Listing 5-12).

Listing 5-12. Template-Driven Forms

```
<form #form="ngForm" (ngSubmit)="loginForm(form)" novalidate>
      <ion-item>
        <ion-label>Login</ion-label>
        <ion-input type="text" required [(ngModel)]="login.username " ngControl="username">
        </ion-input>
      </ion-item>
</form>
```

Class pulls the form values using the reference to the form itself as shown in Listing 5-13.

Listing 5-13. Template-Driven Forms–Class Definition

```
login = {
    username: '',
};
  loginForm(form) {
    console.log(form.value)
  }
```

Forms with FormBuilder

Forms are created in the class and their logic is also maintained in the class. Template should import the FormBuilder from angular/forms. Also, template would use the formGroup and formControlName as shown in Listing 5-14. FormBuilder is a helper service which creates the instance of ControlGroup which we can refer to as "form."

Listing 5-14. FormBuilder-Based Template

```
<form [formGroup]="login" (ngSubmit)="loginForm()">
     <ion-item>
       <ion-label>Login</ion-label>
       <ion-input type="text" formControlName="username"></ion-input>
     </ion-item>
<button type="submit" [disabled]="!login.valid">Submit</button>
   </form>
```

The constructor of the class should declare the FormBuilder group and the form submission can pick up the values from the class variable itself, as shown in Listing 5-15.

Listing 5-15. FormBuilder-Based Class

```
constructor(private fb: FormBuilder) {
this.login = this.fb.group({
     username: ['', Validators.required]
});
  }
  loginForm(){
    console.log(this. login.value)
  }
```

Of the three ways to implement forms, ngModel is simple but has less programmatic control. Forms with Templates is hard to test but easy to develop as it is similar to html forms. The recommended way to implement Forms in Ionic is to follow the FormBuilder, as it's simpler and provides more programmatic control.

Include Weather/Weather Form

In the src/pages/forecast/forecast.html file include the code in Listing 5-16 within the existing <ion-content></ion-content>.

Listing 5-16. Forecast Form

```
<form [formGroup]="forecastForm" novalidate>
     <table width="100%">
       <tr>
       <td>
       <div class="list"> <br>
         <ion-label>Forecast Type</ion-label>
       <ion-list radio-group formControlName="forecastType" name="forecastType">
       <ion-item>
           <ion-label class="item item-radio">daily</ion-label>
           <ion-radio value="daily" checked></ion-radio>
         </ion-item>
         <ion-item>
           <ion-label class="item item-radio">hourly</ion-label>
           <ion-radio value="hourly"></ion-radio>
         </ion-item>
       </ion-list>
     </div>
```

```
      </td>
        <td>
      <ion-item>
          <ion-label floating>Location</ion-label>
          <ion-input type="text" formControlName="location" name="location"></ion-input>
      </ion-item>
      <p [hidden]="forecastForm.controls.location.valid" danger padding-left> Enter a
      valid location</p>

        </td>

      </tr>
      <tr> <td colspan="2">
<button ion-button block [disabled]="!forecastForm.controls.location.valid" (click)="getFore
cast(forecastForm)">
        <ion-icon name="custom-button"></ion-icon>Get Weather</button>
</td> </tr>
        </table>
    </form>
```

A form is a type of FormGroup. A Control is tied to the input field; it has a value and a validation state.

In the code in Listing 5-16, forecastForm is a FormGroup. This form has two fields: a location text field and a radio button group for the forecast type. Based on the validation of location, the message "Enter a valid location" would be displayed. Also, the button to retrieve the weather would be displayed only when the location is valid.

Similarly, the same form fields accept forecast type into the src/pages/weather/weather.html file (Listing 5-17).

Listing 5-17. Weather Form

```
<form [formGroup]="weatherForm" novalidate>
      <table width="100%">
        <tr>
          <td>
      <ion-item>
          <ion-label floating>Location</ion-label>
          <ion-input type="text" formControlName="location" name="location"></ion-input>
      </ion-item> <br>
      <p [hidden]="weatherForm.controls.location.valid" danger padding-left> Enter a valid
      location</p>

        </td>

      </tr>
      <tr> <td> <br>
<button ion-button block [disabled]="!weatherForm.controls.location.valid" (click)="getWeat
her(weatherForm)">
          <ion-icon name="custom-button"></ion-icon>Get Weather</button>
        </td> </tr>
        </table>
    </form>
```

Form Validations in Ionic

Validating the form is an integral part of any application that has form elements. Form validations can be of various types.

- Basic validation. In Ionic this is mostly done using the underlying angular validators.

- Multiple validations. These are allowed for a single form field.

- Custom validations. These can be written using custom validators.

- Server-side validations. This can be done asynchronously by contacting the server.

Validators are used in conjunction with FormBuilder to validate the form fields.

For the basic validation, default *validators* can be used from the @angular/common package. Default validators include the following:

- Validators.required—used for mandatory fields

- Vadliators.maxLength(number)–used to specify the maximum length of the form field

- Vadliators.minLength(number)–used to specify the minimum length of the form field

- Vadliators.pattern('pattern')–used to verify with a *regex* pattern provided

In this chapter we will use all the foregoing default validators in our weather form.

Custom Validations in Ionic

Custom validation can be based on the logic required by the app. It is recommended that you write the custom validations in a separate service. Listing 5-18 provides a sample custom validator which can match the passwords provided in two form fields pwd and confirmPwd.

Listing 5-18. Custom Validator

```
import { Control, ControlGroup } from "@angular/common";

export class CustomValidators {

    public static matchPassword(cg: ControlGroup): { [s: string]: boolean } {
            let pwd = cg.controls[pwd];
    let confirmPwd = cg.controls[confirmPwd];
        if (pwd == confirmPwd ) {
            return { matchPassword: true};
        }
        return null;
    }
}
```

Input to the custom validator may be a Control if the validation is dependent only on one form field, or a ControlGroup if the validation is dependent on more than one form field.

Validation in the Weather Form

The Weather form uses four types of basic validation: required, minimum length, maximum length, and pattern. All four types of validation are applied on the location field. They are applied to the file src/pages/weather/weather.ts via the constructor as shown in Listing 5-19.

Listing 5-19. Constructor of the Weather Form

```
weatherForm: FormGroup;
private appConstants: any;
private Weather: any;
private geometry: any;
private currentWeather: any;
weatherResult: boolean;
summaryIcon: string;

constructor(private navController: NavController, private fb: FormBuilder, appConstants:
AppConstants, WeatherApi: WeatherAPI) {
     this.weatherForm = fb.group({
         'location': ['', Validators.compose([Validators.required,Validators.pattern
         ('[a-zA-Z, ]*'),Validators.minLength(3),Validators.maxLength(100)])]
     });
   this.appConstants = appConstants;
   this.Weather = WeatherApi;
   this.geometry = { "longitude":"", "latitude":""};
   this.currentWeather = {};
   this.weatherResult = false;
   this.summaryIcon ="";
}
```

Include the imports required for the changes added to the constructor as shown in the Listing 5-20. The forecast form requires the same imports.

Listing 5-20. Imports Required for Weather and Forecast Form

```
import { FormBuilder, FormGroup, Validators } from '@angular/forms';
import {AppConstants} from '../../providers/app-constants';
import {WeatherAPI} from '../../providers/weather-api';
```

Similarly, replace the constructor of the src/pages/forecast/forecast.ts file as shown in the Listing 5-21.

Listing 5-21. Constructor of the Forecast Form

```
forecastForm: FormGroup;
 private appConstants: any;
 private Weather: any;
 private geometry: any;
 private minWeather: number[][];
 private maxWeather: number[][];
 private weatherTime: any;
 weatherResult: boolean;
 summaryIcon: string;
```

```
constructor(private navController: NavController, private fb: FormBuilder, appConstants:
AppConstants, WeatherApi: WeatherAPI) {
    this.forecastForm = fb.group({
        'location': ['', Validators.compose([Validators.required,Validators.pattern
        ('[a-zA-Z, ]*'),Validators.minLength(3),Validators.maxLength(100)])],
        'forecastType': 'daily'
    });
    this.appConstants = appConstants;
    this.Weather = WeatherApi;
    this.geometry = { "longitude":"", "latitude":""};
    this.minWeather = new Array();
    this.maxWeather = new Array();
    this.weatherTime = new Array();
    this.weatherResult = false;
    this.summaryIcon ="";
}
```

Add the provider to the component definition, in the src/pages/weather/weather.ts and src/pages/forecast files.

Call the REST Service Provider and Display the Data

Service providers make the REST API and src/pages/weather/weather.ts should call the service provider methods to get the weather (see Listing 5-23).

Listing 5-23. Retrieve Weather Data for Display

```
getWeather(formData: any) {
    this.Weather.getGeometry(this.appConstants.getGoogleAPIURL(), formData.value.location).
    subscribe((data: any) => {
        this.geometry.longitude = data.results[0].geometry.location.lng;
        this.geometry.latitude = data.results[0].geometry.location.lat;
this.Weather.getCurrentWeather(this.geometry.longitude,this.geometry.latitude).
subscribe((weatherData: any) => {
        this.currentWeather=weatherData.currently;
        this.weatherResult = true;
if(this.currentWeather.summary.toLowerCase().indexOf("cloudy") > 0)
        this.summaryIcon = "cloudy";
        else if(this.currentWeather.summary.toLowerCase().indexOf("rainy") > 0)
        this.summaryIcon = "rainy";
        else if(this.currentWeather.summary.toLowerCase().indexOf("sunny") > 0)
        this.summaryIcon = "sunny";
        else if(this.currentWeather.summary.toLowerCase().indexOf("thunderstorm") > 0)
        this.summaryIcon = "thunderstorm";
    });
    });
}
```

getGeometry is called to retrieve the latitude and longitude. Once you have that information you call getCurrentWeather to retrieve the current weather. Icon is also assigned based on the data. Add the code shown in Listing 5-24 at the end of the <ion-content> tag.

Listing 5-24. Update the Weather Display

```
<div *ngIf="weatherResult">
        <h3>Right Now</h3>
        <h2 class="current-temp">
          <ion-icon name="{{summaryIcon}}"></ion-icon>
          {{currentWeather.summary}}&deg;
        </h2>

        <div>
          <div>
            <span>Feels like {{currentWeather.temperature}}</span><br>
            <span>Dew point: {{currentWeather.dewPoint}}</span><br>
            <span>Humidity: {{currentWeather.humidity}}%</span><br>
            <span>Visibility: {{currentWeather.visibility}} mi</span><br>
            <span>Pressure: {{currentWeather.pressure}} mb</span>
          </div>
        </div>
</div>
```

Display the Forecast as Chart

This section focuses on how other modules of angular2 can be integrated with Ionic. To understand this integration, we will use the chart display for the forecast. To display the forecast as a chart, we use the "CHART_DIRECTIVES" from "angular2-highcharts" module. Add the dependency of the angular2-highcharts using the npm with the command shown in Listing 5-25.

Listing 5-25. Charts Plug-in Install

```
$ npm install angular2-highcharts --save
```

Charts are used for the forecast, so let's import the charts into the `src/app/app.module.ts` file as shown in Listing 5-26.

Listing 5-26. Import the Charts Module

```
import { ChartModule } from 'angular2-highcharts';
```

Include the Chartmodule as an import into the `app.module.ts` file (Listing 5-27).

Listing 5-27. Imports in app.module.ts

```
imports: [
    ChartModule,
    IonicModule.forRoot(MyApp)
  ],
```

Include the chart value variable in the `src/pages/forecast/forecast.ts`. Define the variable as part of all the other variable definitions as - `chartValue: {};`

Filtering the JSON retrieved from the forecast API is required for the chart display. JSON filtration retrieves the date/hour details and the temperature details (see Listing 5-28).

Listing 5-28. Filtering of Forecast JSON in src/pages/forecast/forecast.ts

```
filterJson(json,forecastType)
{
    this.minWeather = new Array();
    this.maxWeather = new Array();
    this.weatherTime = new Array();

    for(var i=0;i<json.length;i++)
    {
            var months = ['Jan','Feb','Mar','Apr','May','Jun','Jul','Aug','Sep','Oct','No
v','Dec'];
        var b: Date = new Date(json[i].time * 1000);
        if(forecastType == "daily")
        {
          this.weatherTime.push(b.getDate()+" "+months[b.getMonth()]+" "+b.getFullYear());
          this.maxWeather.push(json[i].temperatureMax);
          this.minWeather.push(json[i].temperatureMin);
        }
        else
        {
          this.weatherTime.push(b.getDate()+" "+months[b.getMonth()]+" "+b.getFullYear() +"
- "+b.getHours() +" hours");
          this.minWeather.push(json[i].temperature);
        }

    }
}
```

To display the chart, JSON filtering has to be called and then passed to the chart options value (see Listing 5-29).

Listing 5-29. Forecast Chart Display in src/pages/forecast/forecast.ts

```
getForecast(formData: any) {
    this.Weather.getGeometry(this.appConstants.getGoogleAPIURL(), formData.value.location).
    subscribe((data: any) => {
      this.geometry.longitude = data.results[0].geometry.location.lng;
      this.geometry.latitude = data.results[0].geometry.location.lat;
      this.Weather.getCurrentWeather(this.geometry.longitude,this.geometry.latitude).
      subscribe((weatherData: any) => {
        this.weatherResult = true;
        if(formData.value.forecastType == "daily")
        {
          this.filterJson(weatherData.daily.data,formData.value.forecastType);
          this.chartValue = {
            title : { text : 'Weather Forecast' },
            chart: { type: 'column' },
            xAxis: {
                    categories: this.weatherTime
                },
            series: [
```

```
                    { name : 'Min Temp', data: this.minWeather},
                    { name : 'Max Temp',  data: this.maxWeather}
                ]
            };
        }
        else
        {
            this.filterJson(weatherData.hourly.data,formData.value.forecastType);
            this.chartValue = {
                title : { text : 'Weather Forecast' },
                chart: { type: 'column' },
                xAxis: {
                            categories: this.weatherTime
                        },
                series: [
                    { name : 'Min Temp', data: this.minWeather},
                ]
            };
        }
    });
    });
}
```

Include the required chart js file into the body of the `src/index.html` file as shown in Listing 5-30.

Listing 5-30. Chart File Included in src/index.html

```
<body>

    <!-- Ionic's root component and where the app will load -->
    <ion-app></ion-app>
    <!-- Chart.js -->
    <script src="https://cdnjs.cloudflare.com/ajax/libs/Chart.js/2.3.0/Chart.min.js"></script>

    <!-- The polyfills js is generated during the build process -->
    <script src="build/polyfills.js"></script>

    <!-- The bundle js is generated during the build process -->
    <script src="build/main.js"></script>

</body>
```

Include the chart tag in the forecast view when the weather result is available at the end `<ion-content>` (Listing 5-31).

Listing 5-31. Include Chart in Forecast View

```
<div *ngIf="weatherResult">
    <chart [options]="chartValue"></chart>
    </div>
```

The code in Listing 5-31 retrieves the forecast data from the REST call and, based on the daily/hourly data, displays the charts.

Run the Weather App

Similarly to what we did in the previous chapters, build and run this app. This app contains two tabs. The first display tab retrieves the current weather, as shown in Figure 5-3.

■ **Note** When you run the app in the browser you may see "No 'Access-Control-Allow-Origin' header is present on the requested resource." To solve this issue, set up a proxy server. To learn more about this issue, refer to http://blog.ionic.io/handling-cors-issues-in-ionic/.

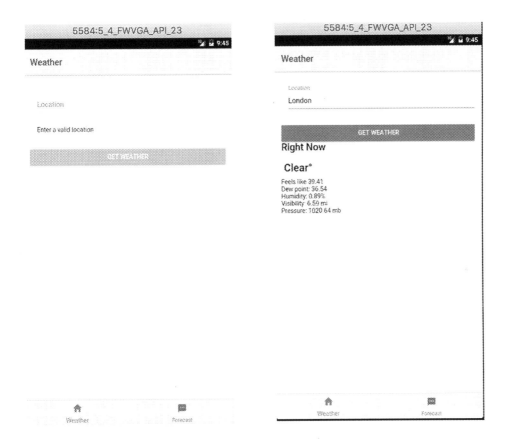

Figure 5-3. First tab view

The second tab displays the weather forecast. It displays the forecast as a chart as in Figure 5-4.

Figure 5-4. *Second tab view—chart view*

MODIFY THE APP TO VALIDATE WEATHER LOCATION

Add a custom validator in to the weather page, for the location to contain some specific starting characters.

Summary

In this chapter, we used the `https://developer.forecast.io/` APIs registration to retrieve the weather data. And, using Ionic, we developed the tab-based app which displays the weather result based on the location entered. In the second tab, the monthly or hourly forecast is displayed as a chart.

CHAPTER 6

Saving Memories

The main objective of Ionic is to help developers build a "native-feeling" app that will run on most of the popular platforms. Ionic native is the wrapper for the Cordova/PhoneGap plug-ins that adds the native features to your mobile app easily. This chapter will help you to use the ionic-native module by employing a camera and storage plug-in

Learning Objectives

- Use camera to snap pictures
- Store the pictures to the device
- Display the pictures in a carousel

What We Will Build

Let's build a "Saving Memories" app, which allows us to capture pictures using the native camera of the mobile device. The app also displays all the pictures in a carousel. This chapter will show you how to store the pictures in the mobile device and details the possible options available for the storage.

Building the App

Create a blank app named "NativeApp." This app is relatively a simple app which uses the camera to snap pictures.

Ionic Native

Ionic Native is a wrapper and adds the native features to the app. This wraps the callback and provides a common interface to all plug-ins. There are 107 native plug-ins listed at `https://ionicframework.com/docs/v2/native/`. To import the plug-ins, a simple import statement would suffice like `import { Camera } from 'ionic-native';`

The required plug-ins have to be installed based on their documentation.

In this chapter we will use the camera and native storage plug-in from this list.

© Josephine Eskaline Joyce Justin and Joesph Xavier Judes 2017
J. Justin and J. Jude, *Learn Ionic 2*, https://doi.org/10.1007/978-1-4842-2617-9_6

Take Pictures

To install the camera plug-in so that it can be used in the app, issue the command from the root folder of the app, as shown in Listing 6-1.

Listing 6-1. Cordova Camera Plug-in Installation

```
$ ionic plugin add cordova-plugin-camera
```

To take pictures, modify the src/pages/home/home.html code to add a button in the nav bar as shown in Listing 6-2. Remove the existing <ion-header> and add the following. Also remove the content inside <ion-content>.

Listing 6-2. Take Pictures Button

```
<ion-header>
  <ion-navbar>
    <ion-title>
      Manage your photos!
    </ion-title>
        <ion-buttons end (click)="takePicture()">
      <button>
        <ion-icon name="camera"></ion-icon>
      </button>
    </ion-buttons>
  </ion-navbar>
</ion-header>
```

To import the camera module to the code, add the code in Listing 6-3 to the src/pages/home/home.ts file.

Listing 6-3. Camera Import

```
import {Camera} from 'ionic-native';
```

takePicture() is the method called when you click the camera button in home.html. Add the method to the src/pages/home/home.ts file as shown in Listing 6-4.

Listing 6-4. Take Picture

```
takePicture(){
    Camera.getPicture({
            quality : 75,
            destinationType : Camera.DestinationType.FILE_URI,
            sourceType : Camera.PictureSourceType.CAMERA,
            allowEdit : true,
            encodingType: Camera.EncodingType.JPEG,
            targetWidth: 300,
            targetHeight: 300,
            saveToPhotoAlbum: false
        }).then((imageUri) => {
          console.log("imageUri is "+imageUri);
    }, (err) => {
        console.log("camera error is"+err);
    });
  }
```

Styles in Ionic2

SASS (Syntactically Awesome Stylesheets) is an extension to CSS (Cascading Style Sheets), which is used in styling the applications. SASS is a CSS pre-processor, which allows developers to write reusable, maintainable, and extensible code in CSS. Version 3 of SASS is SCSS (Sassy CSS), which defines the new syntax for SASS and builds on top of the existing CSS syntax. SCSS is used in Ionic to style the mobile application design.

Following are the few important features of SCSS.

- **Variables**-Variables can be declared and can be reused. For example,

```
$primary : rgb(25,25,25);
h1 {
  color: $primary;
}
```

The variable $primary can be reused in the whole document.

- **Nesting**–Nested selectors inside selectors.

```
page-home {
  .custom-icon {
    font-size: 32px;
    color : blue;
  }
}
```

custom-icon is applicable on the home page only.

- **Extend**–Extend styles from other declarations, which enables us to avoid copying the declarations.

```
.block { margin: 5px 3px; }
h1 {
  @extend .block;
  border: 2px solid #fff;
}
```

- **Mixins**–Mixins are a set of definitions which compiles according to rules or parameters. Create your own functions using Mixins.

```
$font-base: 12px;
@mixin custom-para {
  font-size: $font-base;
}
p {
  @include custom-para;
}
```

- **Import**-@import helps the developer to import partial files. While this provides a small maintainable code set, it also makes an HTTP request to each of these file to include the code.

```
//base1.scss
p {
    margin: 4;
    padding: 0;
}
//base.scss
@import base1;

body {
    font: 100% Palatino;
    background-color: #ffffff;
}
```

Styling the Button

The camera icon is displayed as part of the navigation bar. For better visibility it should be styled to make it little bigger. To add the style, modify the src/pages/home/home.scss file. Add the style in Listing 6-5 as a nested style inside page-home. This is done so that only this page has this style applied.

Listing 6-5. Button Style Change

```
.custom-icon {
  font-size: 32px;
  color : blue;
}
```

To update the icon with the style, update the <ion-buttons> in the pages/home/home.html file as in Listing 6-6.

Listing 6-6. Applying Styled Button

```
<ion-buttons end>
    <button (click)="takePicture()" class="custom-icon">
      <ion-icon name="camera"></ion-icon>
    </button>
  </ion-buttons>
```

Now that we have the "take pictures" functionality, run the app in your device. Figure 6-1 shows the running app. When you click the camera icon, it displays the camera with the options, and the keyboard picture taken.

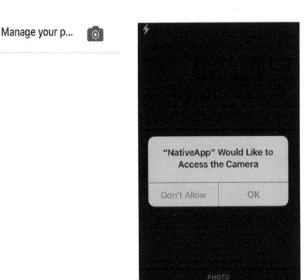

Figure 6-1. *Take picture view*

While running the app, you may see an error: "*Signing for 'NativeApp' requires a development team.*" If so, then open `platforms/ios/NativeApp.xcodeproj` in xcode and assign the profile correctly before you run the app.

Store Pictures

Once a picture is captured, we want to store it. To do this, we can choose to store the list of image URIs (uniform resource identifiers) returned by `takePicture()`. Since it is a list of images, declare an array in the `pages/home/home.ts` file and modify the constructor to initialize the array as shown in Listing 6-7.

Listing 6-7. Array Initialization

```
public base64Image: string[];
  constructor(public navCtrl: NavController) {
    this.base64Image = new Array();
}
```

Modify `takePicture()` to store the URI in the array. Modify the method as shown in Listing 6-8 in the `pages/home/home.ts` file.

Listing 6-8. Store Image URI in the array.

```
takePicture() {
  Camera.getPicture({
        quality : 75,
        destinationType : 1,
        sourceType : Camera.PictureSourceType.CAMERA,
        allowEdit : true,
        encodingType: Camera.EncodingType.JPEG,
```

```
            targetWidth: 300,
            targetHeight: 300,
            saveToPhotoAlbum: false
    }).then((imageUri) => {
        console.log("imageUri is "+imageUri);
        this.base64Image.push(imageUri);
        let imageUris = this.base64Image.map(o => o).join(', ');
        console.log("imageUris is "+imageUris);
}, (err) => {
    console.log("error occurred "+err);
});
}
```

Update the src/pages/home/home.html file to display a message when the array is empty. Add the code in Listing 6-9 within the <ion-content>.

Listing 6-9. Display Message When Image Is Empty

```
<div *ngIf="base64Image.length == 0"> <br/><br/>    Click on the camera icon to
take pictures!</div>
```

Display Pictures

Now that the pictures are stored, let's display the pictures in a carousel. <ion-slides/> are used to display the carousel. Add the code shown in Listing 6-10 within the <ion-content>.

Listing 6-10. Display Pictures

```
<ion-slides pager autoplay="true" pager="true" [options]="extraOptions"  *ngIf="base64Image.
length > 0">
  <ion-slide *ngFor="let image of base64Image">
        <img [src]="image" />
      </ion-slide>
</ion-slides>
```

The ion-slides option has to be defined in the src/pages/home/home.ts file. Define the variable as shown in Listing 6-11.

Listing 6-11. Options Declaration

```
public extraOptions : {};
```

Add the options value, as shown in Listing 6-12, in the constructor of the src/pages/home/home.ts file.

Listing 6-12. Slides Option Values

```
this.extraOptions = {
    pager: true,
    paginationClickable: true,
    spaceBetween: 30,
    centeredSlides: true,
    autoplay: 2000
  }
```

Run the app in a device. Pictures captured using the camera would be displayed as a carousel. But if you switch off the app or close the app and reopen it, the pictures would not be maintained. This is because we are not persisting the image URI. To persist the image URI, we should use any of the storage options available with Ionic.

Ionic Storage

In a mobile device, storage may be required for various reasons, including the following:

- A simple reason that all data need to be stored locally is to prevent external interaction. Json file containing the quotes, which is stored locally in the app is an example.

- Store data locally for specific functionality. The Remember Me app stores the user details locally.

- Cache the data locally to avoid server calls. Server data which does not change often can be stored locally for a specific period.

- Store user preferences locally. An app that gets the user preferences and modifies the app display accordingly can store the user preferences locally.

- Offline data sync requirements can have offline data stored locally. Evernote offline can store the to-dos locally and sync when the device is online.

There are various ways to implement storage in the mobile device. The next few sections discuss the ways to implement storage based on what you are storing.

Local Storage/Web Storage

Local storage and Web storage are simple ways to store the data without any relational database capabilities. Such storage is easy to use and available in both browser-based and hybrid applications. Local storage has a 5 MB data limit which can be extended to 25 MB but can only contain strings. For complex types of data, local storage has to be serialized and lacks performance of complex types of data.

This storage, which is not reliable, should be used only if it's okay to lose the data at any point in time. A few third-party implementations are available for local storage and one of them is localForage.

Native Storage

Native storage is simple and fast persistent storage available for Android, iOS, and Windows applications. Like local storage, this storage is also available only for limited data. But unlike local storage, this storage is persistent and available until the application is removed from the device.

WebSQL

WebSQL provides a way to store data in a structured database which can be queried using SQL syntax. This kind of storage is supported by Android and iOS mobile browsers. This storage supports versioning of data and provides good performance as the data can be indexed.

While not supported by all Cordova platforms, WebSQL is more complex compared to local storage, and WebSQL is deprecated.

SQLLite

SQLLite allows each application in the mobile device to have its own SQL database. Like native storage this is only applicable to mobile applications and not available for HTML5 applications.

SQLite provides a way to persistently store unlimited data which can be managed using SQL syntax.

IndexedDB

This no-SQL approach to the storage is a collection of "object-stores." IndexedDB, supported by Android and Windows (with some limitations), provides better performance than local storage because of its indexing capabilities. Because of its No-SQL approach, Indexed DB provides a more flexible structure of the data. It also supports versioning of data.

Persist the Pictures

To store the image URI persistently, the memories app uses the native storage plug-in of Ionic 2. When pictures are taken, store the image URI in the array. To install the required native plug-in in a terminal, from the root folder of the app, issue the command as shown in Listing 6-13.

Listing 6-13. Import NativeStorage

```
$ ionic plugin add cordova-plugin-nativestorage
```

To import the native storage, modify the existing ionic-native import statement in the src/pages/home/home.ts file as in Listing 6-14.

Listing 6-14. Import NativeStorage

```
import {Camera,NativeStorage} from 'ionic-native';
```

The array should be stored in the native storage. Since NativeStorage can hold only string, the array will be converted into string before storing. Add the code shown in Listing 6-15 to src/pages/home/home.ts after storing the image URI in the array in takePicture().

Listing 6-15. Storing in NativeStorage

```
let imageUris = this.base64Image.map(o => o).join(', '); //This line exist already in the
takePciture()
NativeStorage.setItem('photos', imageUris).then(
        () => console.log('Stored item!'),
        error => console.error('Error storing item', error)
);
```

To use the image URI from NativeStorage, add the code in Listing 6-16 to the constructor. This code splits the stored string into an array.

Listing 6-16. Retrieve from NativeStorage

```
this.platform.ready().then(() => {
  NativeStorage.getItem("photos").then(data => {
                    this.base64Image = data.split(",");
  },
  error => {
    console.log("error in getting photos "+error);
  });
});
```

The code in Listing 6-16 should be called only when the device is ready. `this.platform.ready()` is used to check if the device is ready. Import the platform for this to work. Modify the existing 'ionic-angular' import in Listing 6-17 for the Platform import.

Listing 6-17. Import Platform

```
import { NavController,Platform } from 'ionic-angular';
```

Modify the constructor signature with platform as one of the inputs, as in Listing 6-18.

Listing 6-18. Platform in Constructor

```
constructor(public navCtrl: NavController,  public platform: Platform) { ... }
```

Run the Memories App

As we did in the previous chapters, build and run the app. When the images are empty, the app displays a default message as shown in the Figure 6-2.

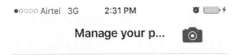

Click on the camera icon to take pictures!

Figure 6-2. Default view

When you click the camera button, it displays the camera and allows the user to capture the pictures as in Figure 6-3.

Figure 6-3. *Camera view*

Once the pictures are being captured, the default view is updated to display the captured images as slides with pagination as shown in Figure 6-4.

Figure 6-4. *Pictures viewed as carousel*

MODIFY THE APP TO PICK UP PHOTOS

Modify this app to include a way to pick up existing photos from the gallery and display them as a carousel in the app.

Summary

In this chapter we looked at camera usage and styling and storage options of Ionic. We created a blank app and added the camera native plug-in to the app. We then used the storage plug-in to store the images' URI to have persistent storage of the photos.

CHAPTER 7

Gather Analytics

Gathering and analyzing mobile app usage data are the key to ascertaining whether the enterprise mobile app is providing required benefits. They are also a key to gaining insights into user sentiments and they help in optimizing the app. This chapter helps in configuring Google analytics with the Ionic app to collect the usage data.

Learning Objectives

- Use the GoogleAnalytics plug-in to gather analytics data
- Understand view tracking and event tracking
- View the results on the Google analytics site

What We Will Build

Let's extend the "Those Famous Quotes" app, to gather analytics data. We will do both the view tracking and event tracking in the app. And we will take a look at the Google analytics charts to analyze the gathered data.

Prerequisite

For using Google analytics we need a GA account, which can be created at `https://analytics.google.com/analytics/web`. In the "Admin" tab, click "create new account" to create a new account for this chapter.

Building the App

"Those Famous Quotes" (QuotesApp) will be enhanced to gather analytics. QuotesApp has two views, a quotes list view and a quotes detail view. These two views will be tracked using Google analytics. Social sharing plug-in is used to share the quote details via Twitter. This event is also gathered as part of the analytics. The Google analytics page displays the number of views of the individual views and the number of shares of the quote.

Install Required Plug-in

We were introduced to Ionic Native in the previous chapter. Google analytics is also integrated with Ionic using the Ionic Native wrapper.

Install the Google plug-in to integrate Google analytics into the app. Following are the different types of analytics you can gather using this plug-in.

- Track a view

- Track an event

- Track a custom metric

- Track exceptions

- Track user timings

- Add transaction data

- Create custom dimensions

- Add user identification

- Mask the IP address (Internet Protocol address)

- App version based analytics

- Enable advertising feature

To find the complete details of this plug-in, refer to `https://ionicframework.com/docs/v2/native/google-analytics/`.

To add the plug-in to the project, issue the following command from the root folder of the project:

```
$ ionic plugin add cordova-plugin-google-analytics
```

Tracking the App

To start tracking the app, include GoogleAnalytics in the app. You can do this at the app level. Update the StatusBar import statement in the following code in the `src/app/app.component.ts` file:

```
import { StatusBar, Splashscreen, GoogleAnalytics } from 'ionic-native';
```

We will use two methods of GoogleAnalytics.

- startTrackerWithId–This is to provide the tracking ID for the project created in the Google Analytics site. This will initiate Google Analytics into the project.

- enableUncaughtExceptionReporting–This is to enable the exception reporting. Those exceptions not caught by the app will be reported. This is an optional step.

Add the code in Listing 7-1 in the `src/app/app.component.ts` file in the constructor inside the `platform.ready()` check.

Listing 7-1. Set the Tracker ID

```
GoogleAnalytics.startTrackerWithId("<tracking id>");
GoogleAnalytics.enableUncaughtExceptionReporting(true).then((_success) => {
console.log("Successful enabling of uncaught exception reporting "+_success)
}).catch((_error) => {
console.log("error occured "+_error)
});
```

■ **Note**   Also add the debug mode to Google Analytics using the code GoogleAnalytics.debugMode(), to debug the analytics gathering.

The tracker ID of the analytics project can be retrieved from the Google Analytics web site. In https://analytics.google.com/analytics/web, select the "Admin" tab. In the Property listing, select the "Tracking Code" link under the "Tracking Info" item as shown in Figure 7-1.

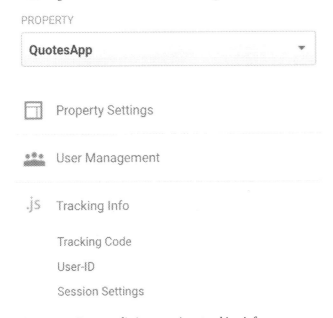

Figure 7-1. Property listing—retrieve tracking info

Tracking Views

To track the number of views on a page, use the trackView() method. Add the code in Listing 7-2 in the constructor of the src/pages/quotes-list/quotes-list.ts file. Add the required import { Platform } from 'ionic-angular';

Listing 7-2. Track View—List

```
platform.ready().then(() => {
GoogleAnalytics.trackView("Quotes List");
});
```

Similar to this, add the code in Listing 7-3 in the src/pages/quotes-detail/quotes-detail.ts file. Add the required import { Platform } from 'ionic-angular';

Listing 7-3. Track View–Details

```
platform.ready().then(() => {
GoogleAnalytics.trackView("Quotes Detail");
});
```

Make sure to import GoogleAnalytics from ionic-native as we did in src/app/app.component.ts.

Tracking Events

To track the events, use the trackEvent() method. In the QuotesApp, which is the base of this AnalyticsApp, a social sharing plug-in is used to share the quotes. If sharing the quotes has to be tracked, add the code in Listing 7-4 to the twitterShare() method in the src/pages/quotes-detail/quotes-detail.ts file.

Listing 7-4. Track View—details

```
let quoteAuthor: string = this.quoteDetail.author;
GoogleAnalytics.trackEvent("Quotes", "Share", quoteAuthor, 1);
```

The trackEvent() method has the following four inputs:

- Category of the event

- Action taken or the event name

- Label for the event

- Numeric value assigned to the event

Run the Analytics App

As you did in the previous chapters, build and run the app in a device. When the Quotes List and Quotes Detail views are initiated, view events are submitted to Google Analytics. Similarly, when the quote sharing is successful, the events are submitted.

If you are in iOS 10 environment, for Google Analytics to work, iAd framework has to be added to your app. Open the built code in Xcode 8.0. In the project ➤ General ➤ Linked Frameworks and Libraries, add the iAd.framework as shown in Figure 7-2.

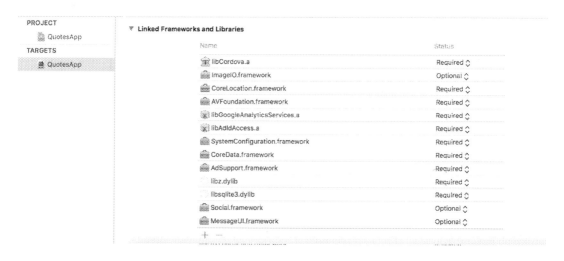

Figure 7-2. *Linked frameworks and libraries*

Click the +button to add the frameworks (Figure 7-3).

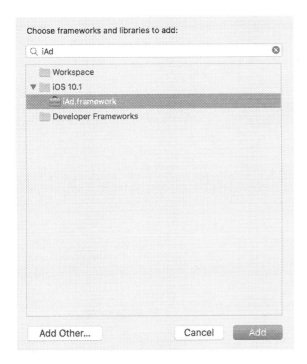

Figure 7-3. *Adding iAd.framework*

Also there may be delay in reporting the events. If your app is up and the Google Analytics is not initialized, wait for a few moments for it to get fully initialized. If your app is reporting the events and if it's not seen in the Google Anlaytics site, wait for a day or so and it will start appearing in the app. For the AnalyticsApp the delay was around 10 minutes.

Google Analytics Charts

The App Overview tab provides the details like users, country, device model, users, and screen details (Figures 7-4 and 7-5). It also provides in-app revenue if the ecommerce tracking is enabled.

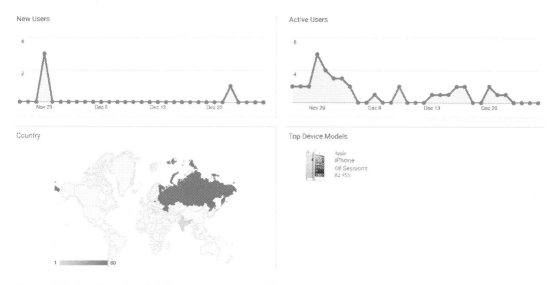

Figure 7-4. *AppOverview details–users, region, and device*

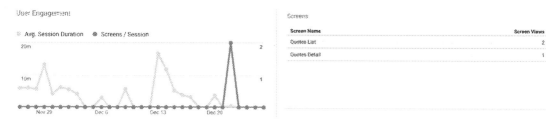

Figure 7-5. *AppOverview details–session details and screens*

Audience ➤ Overview provides details like session duration, demographics, language, and so on (Figure 7-6).

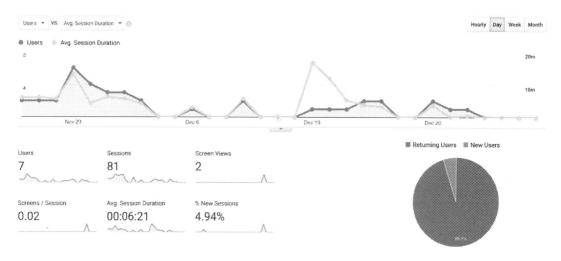

Figure 7-6. *Audience details*

To see the view details, click Behavior ➤ Screens (Figure 7-7).

Figure 7-7. Behavior details–screens

To view the event details, click Behavior ➤ Events ➤ Overview (Figure 7-8).

Figure 7-8. Behavior details–events

Real-time details can be collected like how many users are currently using the app. To collect real-time details, use the real-time category as shown in Figure 7-9.

Figure 7-9. *Real-time view*

MODIFY THE APP TO ADD MORE ANALYTICS DATA

Modify this app to include custom metric and transactions, and view them on the Google Analytics site.

Summary

In this chapter we enabled Google Analytics for the QuotesApp, which can track views and events using the Google Analytics native plug-in. We ran the app in a device, and for every view of the two screens in the app, analytics is hit. Also we learned that different views of the Google Analytics site display various analytics information about the app.

CHAPTER 8

Go Offline

Users of any data-driven mobile application should be able to read and write data without an Internet connection. When the app reconnects to the Internet, the details should be synced to the server. In this chapter we will build an offline mobile app that stores data locally and syncs with an actual database (db) when the connectivity is available.

Learning Objectives

- Use Pouch DB, a JavaScript DB, with Ionic which syncs with a hosted DB
- Use IBM Cloudant DB, a NoSQL hosted DB from IBM
- Code a mobile application which will sync with a hosted DB

What We Will Build

We will build a to-do app to which we can add to-dos. These individual to-do items will be stored in the Cloudant db. If the device is offline or has no connectivity with the Cloudant db, then the local db is stored with the updates. Data sync occurs when the Cloudant db becomes available.

Prerequisite

For this chapter we need a Cloudant account and a db created for this tutorial.

Cloudant Account Creation

To create an account, you can generate a service in Bluemix. Refer to `https://console.ng.bluemix.net/catalog/services/cloudant-nosql-db` for more information on Bluemix.

You can also create the account directly at `http://cloudant.com`. Following are the steps to create an account `@Cloudant.com`:

- In a browser, visit `http://cloudant.com`.
- Click the Sign Up button
- On the "Sign Up for a Free Account" page, provide the required details and click the Create my Account button.

You have successfully created your account!

© Josephine Eskaline Joyce Justin and Joesph Xavier Judes 2017
J. Justin and J. Jude, *Learn Ionic 2*, https://doi.org/10.1007/978-1-4842-2617-9_8

Create To-Do Database

To create a database, log in to Cloudant.com with the user ID details provided previously. Based on the username that you used during the registration, the URL (uniform resource locator) to the Cloudant db would be `http://<user name provided during registration>.cloudant.com/dashboard`.

To create a database, click "Create Database" and provide a name, as shown in Figure 8-1. For this tutorial, we will use the db name "tododb."

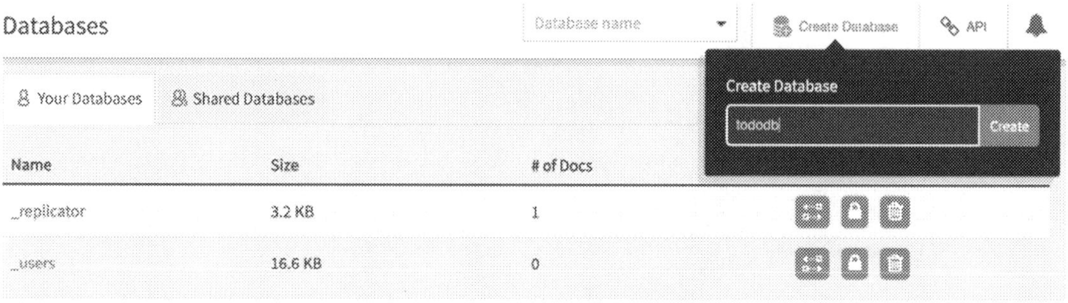

Figure 8-1. *Cloudant db creation*

Building the App

As in previous chapters, create a new Ionic project using the ionic start command shown in Listing 8-1 and name the project "OfflineToDo."

Listing 8-1. Start Blank Project

```
$ ionic start OfflineToDo blank --v2 --ts
```

Introduction to PouchDB

PouchDB is an in-browser counterpart to CouchDB. It provides an easy way to replicate the data from a remote db. Following are the features of PouchDB:

- In-Browser db–Pouch DB can run in various browsers and helps to execute queries faster, as there is no need to execute queries over network.

- Lightweight–It is a very lightweight db, which can be installed using scripts even in mobile devices.

- Easy to implement—It is a JavaScript-based db and is easy to implement.

- Open Source–It is an open source-based db.

- Document-based database—data is stored in granular data types, with associative mapping of keys to documents.

Introduction to IBM Cloudant DB

IBM Cloudant DB is a managed NoSQL JSON database. Following are the features of IBM Cloudant DB:

- Global Availability–Cloudant supports horizontal scalling which helps users connect to the closest copy of the data, which in turn reduces latency.

- Flexibility–Data is accessible as JSON and provides schema flexibility.

- Offline apps–Cloudant Sync provides a better, faster user experience.

Every document in Cloudant DB contains an _id field. This field identifies the document in a database which is unique. When adding a new document, it can be specified manually or automatically generated. Cloudant also contains a _rev field, which holds the revision number of the document and changes each time a document is modified.

How Offline Sync Works

The offline sync feature helps store and retrieve data on or from local or remote storage. Figure 8-2 shows the sync architecture between devices.

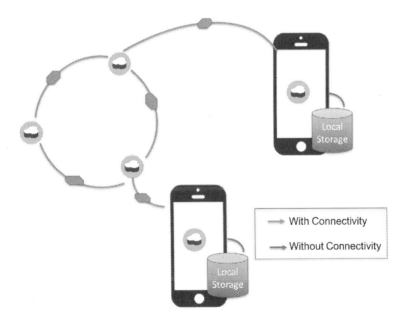

Figure 8-2. *Offline sync architecture*

Install Required Modules

Go to the OfflineToDo project folder and install Pouch DB using npm as shown in Listing 8-2.

Listing 8-2. Install Pouch DB

```
$ npm install pouchdb
```

Add a Data Service

Add a provider named "dataservice" in to the OfflineToDo project as shown in Listing 8-3. This provider will contain the db-related code.

Listing 8-3. Dataservice Generation

```
$ ionic generate provider dataservice
```

As we need pouchdb and promise for database-related implementation, import the required ones in the src/providers/dataservice.ts file (Listing 8-4).

Listing 8-4. Required Import for dataservice

```
import PouchDB from 'pouchdb';
import 'rxjs/add/operator/toPromise';
```

To Do service doesn't need any http import. So import { Http } from '@angular/http'; can be removed from this file.

To add the Cloudant db-related information, define the required variables and initialize the db in the constructor. Add the code from Listing 8-5 inside the Dataservice class, replacing the constructor code.

Listing 8-5. Db Initialization

```
private db: any ;
//cloudant username
private userName = 'XYZ';
//cloudant password
private password= 'XYZ' ;
//cloudant db url
private dbURL = 'https://XYZ.cloudant.com/tododb';
//array of todos
private toDos = [];

constructor() {
  this.db = new PouchDB('tododb');
    let options = {
      live: true,
      retry: true,
      continuous: true,
      auth: {
        username: this.userName,
        password: this.password
      }
    }
    //Sync the db with Cloudant
    this.db.sync(this.dbURL, options);
}
```

When the app is initialized, the dataservice constructor is called which will sync the local db with the remote db.

To add and delete ToDo items add the respective data service methods in the Dataservice class as shown in the Listing 8-6.

Listing 8-6. Add and Delete

```
addToDo(doc) {
        return this.db.post(doc);
}

deleteToDo(doc) {
        return this.db.remove(doc);
}
```

To retrieve Todo items, add the method shown in Listing 8-7. This method returns a promise which has the "toDos" as an array. Also if the data is changed, it will call the method onChange to update the data accordingly.

Listing 8-7. Retrieve To Do

```
retrieveToDos(){
        return new Promise<any>(resolve => {

                this.db.allDocs({include_docs: true}).then((result) => {
                        if (result.total_rows > 0)
                        {
                                result.rows.map((row) => {
                                        this.toDos.push(row.doc);
                                        resolve(this.toDos);
                                });
                        }
                        else {
                                resolve(this.toDos);
                        }
                        this.db.changes({live: true, since: 'now', include_docs: true}).
                        on('change', (change) => {
                                this.onChange(change);
                        });
                }).catch((error) => {
                        console.log(error);
                });
        });
}
```

If the data is updated, we need to update the toDos array accordingly. So the onChange method in Listing 8-8 accordingly updates by checking the modified doc and the index.

Listing 8-8. Handle Data Changes

```
onChange(change){
        let changedDoc = null;
        let changedIndex = null;
        this.toDos.forEach((doc, index) => {
                if(doc._id === change.id){
```

```
                              changedDoc = doc;
                              changedIndex = index;
                   }
        });

        //Handle deleted document
        if(change.deleted){
                   this.toDos.splice(changedIndex, 1);
        }
        else {
                   //Handle the updates
                   if(changedDoc){
                              this.toDos[changedIndex] = change.doc;
                   }
                   //Handle additions
                   else {
                              this.toDos.push(change.doc);
                   }
        }
}
```

Now that we have the data service layer ready, it's time to work on the view part.

Listing To Do

The initial view of the app displays the To Do list. To retrieve the list, add the code in Listing 8-9, replacing the constructor in the src/pages/home/home.ts file.

Listing 8-9. Retrieve the To Do for Updating the View

```
public toDos : any[];
public noToDo : boolean;
constructor(private todoService: Dataservice, private navController: NavController, private
platform: Platform) {
        this.navController = navController;
        this.platform.ready().then(() => {
                   this.todoService.retrieveToDos().then(data => {
                              this.toDos = data;
                              if(this.toDos.length > 0 ) {
                                this.noToDo = false;
                              }
                              else {
                                this.noToDo = true;
                              }
                   })
                   .catch(console.error.bind(console));
        });
}
```

Add the required import as shown in Listing 8-10 for the code in Listing 8-9.

Listing 8-10. Required home.ts Import

```
import {NavController, Platform} from 'ionic-angular';
import {Dataservice} from '../../providers/dataservice';
```

To add the dataservice as a provider, add the code in Listing 8-11 into the @Component part.

Listing 8-11. Add the Provider

```
@Component({
  selector: 'page-home',
  templateUrl: 'home.html',
  providers: [Dataservice]
})
```

Update the user identification (UI) to display the list of To Do. Replace with the code in Listing 8-12 in src/pages/home/home.html. Besides displaying the list, this code also has a button to display a To Do addition page. Each To Do that is being displayed also displays a sliding option on the right side. This sliding option provides a way to delete the To Do.

Listing 8-12. View Update to List To Do

```
<ion-header>
  <ion-navbar>
    <ion-title>
      To Do
    </ion-title>
    <ion-buttons end>
      <button (click)="showToDoPage()">
          <ion-icon name="add"></ion-icon>
      </button>
    </ion-buttons>
  </ion-navbar>
</ion-header>

<ion-content class="home">
    <div *ngIf="noToDo">
      <br/>Click on + to add to do items.
    </div>

    <ion-list inset>
    <ion-item-sliding *ngFor="let toDo of toDos" >
        <ion-item>
          <h2>{{ toDo.name }} -  {{ toDo.createdTime | date:'yMMMMd' }}</h2>
          <p class="item-description">{{toDo.description}}</p>
        </ion-item>
        <ion-item-options side="right">
          <button ion-button (click)="delete(toDo)">
```

```
          <ion-icon name="ion-trash-a"></ion-icon>
          Delete
        </button>
      </ion-item-options>
  </ion-item-sliding>
      </ion-list>
</ion-content>
```

To quickly test the main view, run the app using 'ionic serve.' This will run the app in the browser. The To Do list would be empty except for the Add button (to add the To Do) and a message as shown in Figure 8-3.

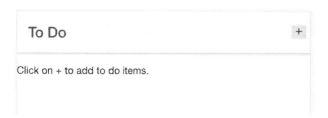

Figure 8-3. *Empty To Do*

You will notice a "No 'Access-Control-Allow-Origin' header is present on the requested resource" error when you run the app at this stage. Setting up a proxy to handle CORS (Cross-Origin Resource Sharing) issues is the right way to solve this problem. Since we will ultimately run it on the device, for now run the browser without any security like "./Google\ Chrome --disable-web-security --user-data-dir".

Adding To Do

Add a new page for adding To Do using ionic generate (Listing 8-13).

Listing 8-13. Adding 'Add To Do' Page

```
$ ionic generate page addtodo --ts
```

Since we need the dataservice, as we did in the src/pages/home/home.ts file, import the dataservice and also include the provider in the @Component in the file src/pages/addtodo/addtodo.ts.

Import the required FormBuilder, FormGroup, and Validators for the To Do form implementation (Listing 8-14).

Listing 8-14. Form-Related Import

```
import { FormBuilder, FormGroup, Validators } from '@angular/forms';
```

Replace the constructor of the addtodo.ts file with the code in Listing 8-15.

Listing 8-15. Form Validation

```
todoForm: FormGroup;
constructor(private navController: NavController, private fb: FormBuilder, private
todoService: Dataservice) {
     this.todoForm = fb.group({
       'name': ['', Validators.compose([Validators.required,Validators.pattern
       ('[a-zA-Z, ]*'),Validators.minLength(3),Validators.maxLength(100)])],
       'description':['']
     });
  }
```

Add the form elements and the submit button for adding the To Do in src/pages/addtodo/addtodo.
html. Replace the contents with the code in Listing 8-16.

Listing 8-16. Add To Do View

```
<ion-header>
  <ion-navbar>
    <ion-title>Add To Do</ion-title>
  </ion-navbar>
</ion-header>
<ion-content padding>
  <form [formGroup]="todoForm" (ngSubmit)="addToDo()">
    <ion-list>
      <ion-item>
        <ion-label color="primary">Name</ion-label>
        <ion-input placeholder="Name" formControlName="name"></ion-input>
      </ion-item>

      <ion-item>
        <ion-label color="primary">Description</ion-label>
        <ion-input placeholder="Description" formControlName="description" ></ion-input>
      </ion-item>

      <ion-item>
        <button ion-button block [disabled]="!todoForm.valid" type="submit">
        Add To Do</button>
      </ion-item>
    </ion-list>
    </form>
</ion-content>
```

When you click the Add To Do button, addToDo() is called. This method has to be added to the
addtodo.ts file. Add the code in Listing 8-17 inside the AddtodoPage class.

Listing 8-17. Add To Do Method

```
addToDo() {
        let date = new Date();
        let newDoc = {
                'name': this.todoForm.value.name,
                'description':this.todoForm.value.description,
                'createdTime': date.getTime()
        };
        //Add the to do using the data service
        this.todoService.addToDo(newDoc);
        //After the addition navigate to the list view
        this.navController.popToRoot();
}
```

Now that we have all the required code to add To Do, we need to add the code to navigate from the home.html page to the addtodo.html page. In the `src/pages/home/home.html` file, we already called the `showToDoPage()` to display the Add page. This method would contain the code for the navigation as shown in Listing 8-18.

Listing 8-18. Navigate to Add To Page

```
showToDoPage() {
        this.navController.push(AddtodoPage);
}
```

This page has to be added as part of the import by adding `import { AddtodoPage } from '../pages/addtodo/addtodo';`.

Finally, the app module has to be modified to include the new addtodo page. For including the page, open the `src/app/app.module.ts` file. Add the import of the addtodo page-`import { AddtodoPage } from '../pages/addtodo/addtodo';`.

Also, in the list of declarations and entryComponents, add the AddtodoPage. The final content of the `app.module.ts` file should look like the code in Listing 8-19.

Listing 8-19. App Module Content

```
import { NgModule, ErrorHandler } from '@angular/core';
import { IonicApp, IonicModule, IonicErrorHandler } from 'ionic-angular';
import { MyApp } from './app.component';
import { HomePage } from '../pages/home/home';
import { AddtodoPage } from '../pages/addtodo/addtodo';

@NgModule({
  declarations: [
    MyApp,
    HomePage,
    AddtodoPage
  ],
```

```
  imports: [
    IonicModule.forRoot(MyApp)
  ],
  bootstrap: [IonicApp],
  entryComponents: [
    MyApp,
    HomePage,
    AddtodoPage
  ],
  providers: [{provide: ErrorHandler, useClass: IonicErrorHandler}]
})
export class AppModule {}
```

Deleting To Do

You have already added a sliding option to delete a To Do in the home.html file; the sliding option displays the Delete button which, when clicked, will call the delete method. The method shown in Listing 8-20 should be added to the src/pages/home/home.ts file.

Listing 8-20. Delete To Do

```
delete(item) {
      this.todoService.deleteToDo(item);
}
```

Run the To Do App

To run the app on a device or an emulator, build and run the app. We will test the sync by running the app with and without connectivity to verify the behavior of offline sync.

Running the App with Connectivity

To test the sync between two devices run the app on two different devices. Adding the To Do item on one of the devices also updates the other device due to the sync feature.

The initial view on both the devices shows empty To Do items (see Figure 8-4).

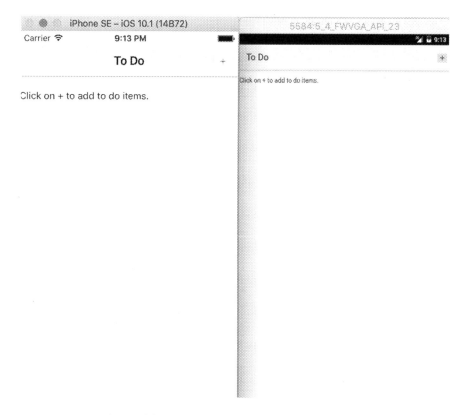

Figure 8-4. *Initial view of the app*

Add an item to one of the devices as shown in Figure 8-5.

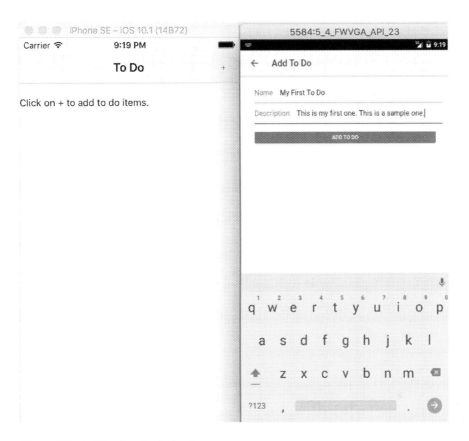

Figure 8-5. *Adding item in device 1*

Once you submit the To Do, it updates the other device immediately as both are connected (see Figure 8-6).

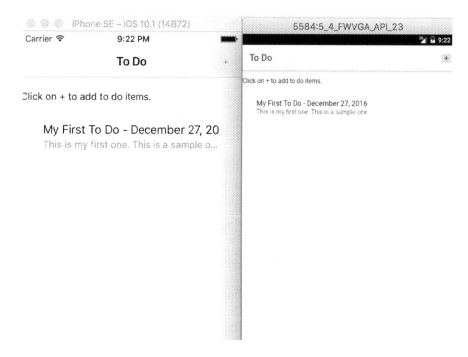

Figure 8-6. *Item on device 1 updates the other device list too*

Similarly, adding a new To Do item on device 2 updates both the devices. Add a To Do on the other device as shown in Figure 8-7.

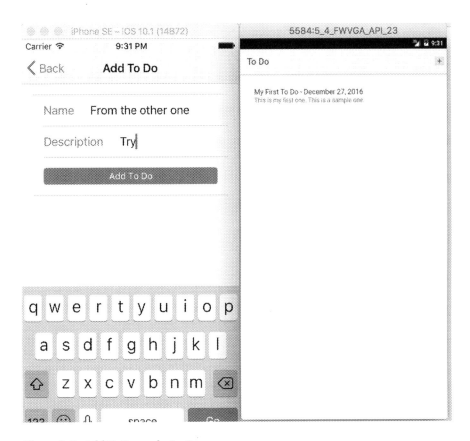

Figure 8-7. *Add To Do on device 2*

Now both the devices display the To Do list that has been added (see Figure 8-8).

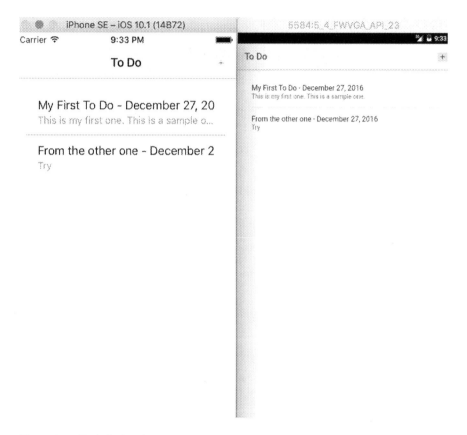

Figure 8-8. *Both devices in sync*

Running the App Without Connectivity

Run one of the devices in airplane mode or remove the connectivity and add a To Do item. In Figure 8-9 one of the devices shows the airplane symbol to indicate that it is not connected to the Internet.

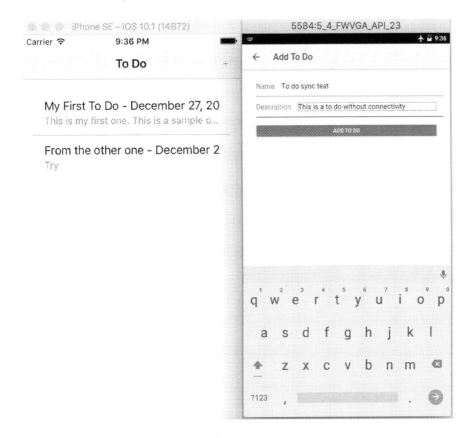

Figure 8-9. *Add To Do in airplane mode*

Because the device did not have connectivity, the To Do item is stored only in local storage and did not update the Cloudant db (i.e., sync did not happen). So both devices show a different list of To Do items, as in Figure 8-10.

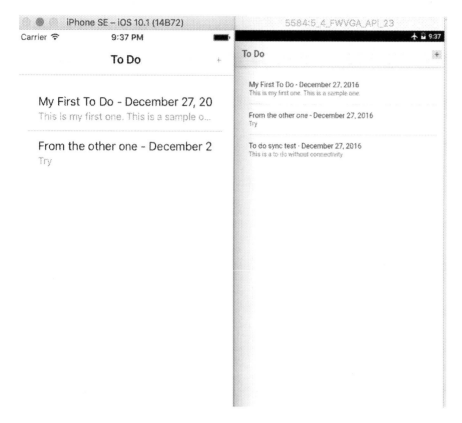

Figure 8-10. *No connectivity, no sync*

Now turn off airplane mode and reconnect to the Internet. You can see that the other device updates immediately, as shown in Figure 8-11.

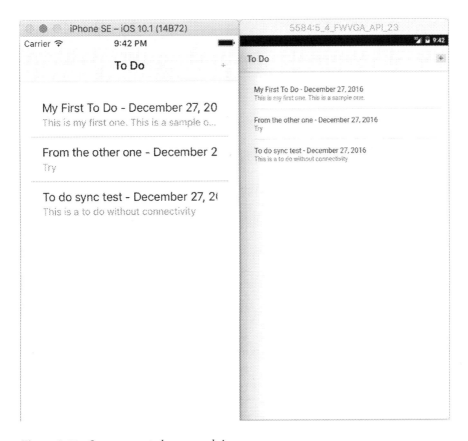

Figure 8-11. Once connected, sync works!

MODIFY THE APP TO UPDATE TO DO ITEMS

Modify this app to include updates to the to do items using a sliding option and required dataservice layer methods.

Summary

In this chapter, we installed the pouch db plug-in and used it to create a to-do list. When you connect the device to the Internet, the To Do list is synced to the db and all the devices running the app get the new items. To Do lists are stored in the Cloudant db when connectivity exists. When the device is not connected to the Internet, the added item is stored in the local pouch db and then syncs to Cloudant db when the Internet becomes available.

CHAPTER 9

Where to Go From Here

We learned a lot of important concepts about Ionic 2 in this book. In this chapter we will discuss Ionic 2 tools and services and becoming part of the Ionic community.

Learning Objectives

- Discover additional Ionic 2 tools and services
- Become part of Ionic 2 community

Additional Ionic 2 Tools and Services

In addition to the framework, the Ionic team has created many tools to ease the development of mobile apps. Let us look at some of them.

Ionic Creator

Ionic creator is a drag-and-drop prototyping tool to create mobile apps quickly. You can create a new account at `https://creator.ionic.io/`. Once you create an account and sign in, you can generate new projects by choosing a template. The options are similar to the ones offered in Ionic CLI. After you select a template, you will be greeted with a screen similar to the one in Figure 9-1.

© Josephine Eskaline Joyce Justin and Joesph Xavier Judes 2017
J. Justin and J. Jude, *Learn Ionic 2*, https://doi.org/10.1007/978-1-4842-2617-9_9

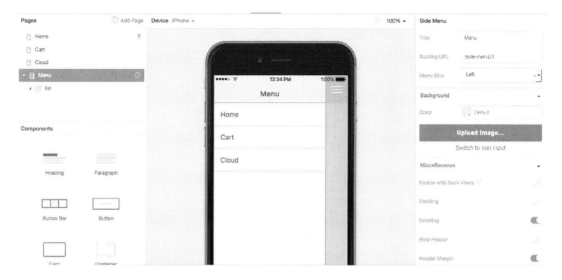

Figure 9-1. *Ionic Creator*

From here, you can add pages (screens) to your app, add UI (user interface) elements to pages, and save and export your files. You can use these files from your desktop for further coding.

Ionic View

You have developed your mobile app and tested it, and you see that it works well on your devices. Now what? Next you want to distribute the app to beta testers.

You could go through the long AppStore approval process, or you could distribute the app through Ionic View app. If you are familiar with iOS development, the Ionic View app is similar to TestFlight.

You can download the Ionic app from `http://view.ionic.io/`.

Ionic Cloud

Ionic cloud is a mobile back-end service providing push notification, user authentication, and packaging of mobile apps into native apps. Ionic offers this in a "freemium" model, which has free monthly quotas. So you can develop it for free and even use it for free until your user base grows. You can learn about Ionic Cloud and its pricing at `https://ionic.io/cloud`.

Ionic Marketplace

Are you building an e-commerce app? Do you want to display charts in your hybrid mobile app? Ionic marketplace hosts community-developed plug-ins, themes, and starter kits to speed up your Ionic project. It has both free and paid versions. You should be able to find a suitable asset for your project.

You can also host your assets on the marketplace. You can host your assets for free and get exposure or you can sell them and earn. The choice is yours.

You can learn about Ionic Marketplace at `https://market.ionic.io/`.

Ionic Community

Every component of Ionic 2 is evolving fast, like TypeScript, Angular, and Ionic itself. The success of any platform depends on its community, and the Ionic team has ensured that the community grows continuously.

The traditional community, Ionic Forum (`https://forum.ionicframework.com`), is a typical Q & A site dedicated to Ionic. You can post your questions and receive answers.

There is also a slack community. You can sign up for this community at `http://ionicworldwide.herokuapp.com/`. There you can showcase your apps, post questions, and also interact with other Ionic developers around the world. This community is more informal than the other options.

You can use Stackoverflow to get answers regarding technical questions. If you have questions specific to Ionic 2, follow `http://stackoverflow.com/questions/tagged/ionic2`.

Codepen is a site where you can learn everything about the front end via code sharing. You can also post your code and share it with others. Codepen has an exclusive page for Ionic at `https://codepen.io/ionic/`.

Similar to Codepen, there is an Ionic playground at `http://play.ionic.io/`. You can code specific parts of an Ionic app and share that piece of app with others. You can use both Codepen and Ionic playground to test pieces of your app.

As a platform, Ionic ecosystem is also growing. Check out the latest partners in the ecosystem at the Ionic home page (`http://ionicframework.com/`)

Summary

Ionic is not just a mobile framework. It is a rich ecosystem for mobile developers. It has a tool for every phase of the mobile development life cycle. You can mock up screens with Ionic creator, get a head start with themes and plug-ins from the Ionic marketplace, develop the mobile app with the Ionic framework, get feedback from testers using Ionic View, and continue to update your app with Ionic cloud.

In this book, we learned to develop fully featured hybrid mobile applications using the Ionic framework. We also learned about other tools in the Ionic ecosystem. Now go create awesome mobile applications using Ionic and grab the attention of the world. Best wishes.

Erratum to: Learn Ionic 2

Joyce Justin and Joseph Jude

Erratum to:

J. Justin and J. Jude, *Learn Ionic 2,* **https://doi.org/10.1007/978-1-4842-2617-9**

The book was inadvertently published with an incorrect copyright holder of captioned title as "The Editor(s) (if applicable) and The Author(s)" whereas it should be "Josephine Eskaline Joyce Justin and Joesph Xavier Judes". The copyright holder has been updated in the book.

The updated original online version for this book can be found at
https://doi.org/10.1007/978-1-4842-2617-9

© Josephine Eskaline Joyce Justin and Joesph Xavier Judes 2018
J. Justin and J. Jude, *Learn Ionic 2*, https://doi.org/10.1007/978-1-4842-2617-9_10

Index

© Josephine Eskaline Joyce Justin and Joesph Xavier Judes 2017
J. Justin and J. Jude, *Learn Ionic 2*, https://doi.org/10.1007/978-1-4842-2617-9

▓ U, V

▓ W, X, Y, Z

Get the eBook for only $5!

Why limit yourself?

With most of our titles available in both PDF and ePUB format, you can access your content wherever and however you wish—on your PC, phone, tablet, or reader.

Since you've purchased this print book, we are happy to offer you the eBook for just $5.

To learn more, go to http://www.apress.com/companion or contact support@apress.com.

Apress®

Printed in the United States
By Bookmasters